It's All Bad

Street Dreams

by Qew

Dedication

I dedicate this book to my first son, Quint, who continues to inspire, push and motivate me. This one is for you.

When I first started this process over 12 years ago, it was simply to pass the time. Fast-forward to the beginning of this year, 2026," I actually began to get a glimpse at how much time and effort go into transforming words that were written on a legal pad into an actual published book. It's been a journey worth taking, I must say. Some parts of it I wouldn't take again, yet, at the same time, I'm glad I did. Now that I'm on the other side, I can give thanks to those who helped, loved, encouraged, and supported me through the dark days, long nights, and uncharted territories that I traveled to get to where I am today.

With that being said, I choose to begin with the woman who showed me how to end this dream of publishing my first book by turning it into reality. Donna Christopher, you're an angel in the rarest form. Thank you for taking the time to work with me, for your dedication and expertise, for sharing your wisdom, and for all of your advice. Without you, I'd still be rubbing my head and pinching the bridge of my nose, wondering how I would ever get published. Thank you, thank you, thank you, and I can't wait to work with you again.

The next person I'd like to thank is Marquis "Pooh" Dunn. I don't think you signed up to be my mentor, but I'm here now informing you that is exactly what you've been. I know that you truly believe in the saying, "Each one, teach one," and I'm glad to say that I've learned a lot through this process from you. Our talks, and the time you took out of your days, will never be overlooked. You've kept it solid since the day I first met you, over a few decades ago. Thanks, Pooh, for remaining real and passing me the game.

Candace Williams Bradley and MaKayla Renee Perrien, you two are natural-born helpers. The two of you, alone, I feel, could fix the world, and will help just about anyone in it if they would just ask. I'm so, so, so, so, so glad that y'all are my cousins. (Ok, Candace, we know you're more like my sister, but you know what I'm saying.) Without you two assisting me in getting copies made, reading and rereading the book, helping me send money where it needed to go, and so much more. I'd still be dreaming. Thank y'all so much. I love y'all to the end of time and into the next lifetime.

To my wonderful, loving, and supportive family who play a huge role, and help to round off the cast of people that I could not have done this without. I love y'all, and thank you for believing in me.

To my mother, Bessie Williams, and my sons, Omar McLaurine and Jer'Mar'Reon Tucker, I love y'all with the heart of God! A special thanks, I feel, is due to my two oldest cousins, Michael Davis and Marlo Angelic Davis, for always stepping up and stepping in to help my mother and kids out when I'm not able.

Calvin Howse, Jason McCullough, Terrell Holt, Chance Vaughn, Michael Ingram, Lonnell Foster, and those that are gone but will never be forgotten, Dwayne Falls, Charles 'TJ' Williams, and James Nicholson, nothing happens for nothing. We know where we come from and what we've been through. I could say so much more, but we'll just leave it at that, love y'all.

I've always heard that patience is a virtue, and "It's All Bad" is the product of this saying. Thanks to those that I mentioned, the ones that I didn't, and the ones that doubted, which drove me to keep going. It's time to stop waiting and start reading.

God, I'm so grateful to be living in Your grace and have witnessed, and continue to witness, Your mercy. You placed everyone in the right place at the right time, allowing me to receive from them the experience, knowledge, assistance, and love I needed to create what the person reading this is seeing right now.

To you, the reader, thank you and enjoy!

It's All Bad

Street Dreams

Chapter 1
Get Yo Ass Up!

DeJuan was lost in a dream and, for the death of him, he couldn't wake up. He was drowning, and what made it worse was the fact that his son, Lil D, was drowning too. Lil D was a spitting image of him, and DeJuan was the type of father who would do anything for his child. Hearing Lil D call out, "Daddy-daddy," and not being able to do anything to help, was the worst part of the dream.

DeJuan was scared for his life and his son's life. He kept hearing Lil D's voice cry out to him until he finally pulled himself from the dream. Now awake, he realized Lil D was sitting on his chest, and orange juice was spilled all over his face in an attempt to wake him. He couldn't even be mad after seeing the smile on his son's face. All he could do was shake his head.

After shaking the last few thoughts of the nightmare from his mind, DeJuan playfully said, "Wat up, lil dude… you tryna kill me?"

Lil D looked at him, confused, shook his head from side to side, and said, "Naw, daddy. Momma da one told me to wake you up. She in dere cooking."

DeJuan could smell the bacon. He lifted Lil D from his chest and placed him on the floor so he could grab the basketball shorts he had on before getting into bed the night before. He and his girlfriend, TyChelle, Lil D's mother, had a "no clothes" policy when it came to getting into bed. Before getting up, he slid his shorts on under the covers.

After slipping his feet into his Nike slides, he and his twin struck out, followed their noses downstairs, through the living room, and towards the kitchen.

TyChelle could see them coming. "I hope my two favorite men are hungry," she said.

Lil D, once again, looked confused. "Momma, I been dun said I was hungry, and you said you was gon make me some flat cakes."

TyChelle and DeJuan looked at each other and smiled, and she asked, "Daddy, you want anything special? I got you some grits on already, and when this last pancake gets done, I'm gon whip up some eggs and cheese. Tha bacon already done."

"Naw, Ma. You did yo thang this morning. Wat's tha occasion?" DeJuan said, reaching into the cabinet for the plates to set the table.

"You told me not to let you sleep too late today, said you needed to take care of some business or something. I figured if you had a full day ahead of you, you might as well start it with a full stomach."

DeJuan placed the plates on the table, walked up behind TyChelle, and said into her ear, "And dat's why I love you, bae," before smacking her on her ass.

"So does that mean I ain't gon be last on tha list to get my shit? Cause I got some things to do too," TyChelle said, stacking pancakes onto the plates.

He grabbed the orange juice from the refrigerator, then looked at her and said, "You'll never be last in my book, love."

"Well, ain't you sweet this morning, but I'm serious, Dee. I gotta get my hair, nails, and toes did today. Can you take Lil D to get a haircut cause I gotta take a couple thangs to Crissy when I'm through at tha shop?" TyChelle said as she finished fixing everybody's plate and taking her seat at the table.

"What… you don't think I'm serious?" he said, stuffing his mouth with bacon and eggs. "Yeah, I'll take him with me to the barbershop. But you gotta get him after you holla at ya girl."

"Aite," she said, while watching Lil D demolish his pancakes. She asked Lil D, "You wanna go wit yo daddy to tha barbershop?"

Lil D kept digging into his pancakes like he was trying to win a blue ribbon.

"Lil D!" TyChelle raised her voice, startling him. "You act like you ain't had food before. I said, you wanna go wit your daddy?"

Lil D looked at her with syrup on his chin and said, "I ain't had none today."

"Okay, boy. You got some now. So, you wanna go with your daddy?"

"Yeah, when I get through wit my flat cakes," he said, mopping syrup up with a pancake before shoving it into his mouth.

TyChelle and DeJuan both shook their heads.

"You gotta eat your bacon and eggs too if you wanna go wit me." DeJuan said, finishing the last of his eggs and grits, then standing with his glass of orange juice in his hand.

"I am, daddy, but I gotta eat my flatcakes first cause dey tha best," Lil D said, looking exactly like his daddy.

"Aite. Wateva you say, lil dude. When you get through, go find you something to wear so you can take a bath before we go," DeJuan said.

He watched TyChelle roll her eyes. She thought about Lil D picking through his drawers looking for whatever he thought he was going to put on, while making a mess for her to straighten up once they left.

DeJuan threw on some True Religion shorts, a white T-shirt, with some white Air Force 1's. Lil D chose to put on some blue jean shorts with rips in them, his favorite gray and blue Nike shirt, and his navy-blue Nike Cortezes.

When they made it to the barbershop, Lil D had the attention of everyone in the building, and he loved it, as always.

As soon as they stepped through the door, Faye stopped arching a girl's eyebrows to give Lil D a hug and five dollars. "Com'mere Lil D… where you been? Why you ain't been to see me?" she said, squeezing him tightly.

The girl in Faye's chair looked down at him, "He's so handsome." Then she looked over at DeJuan and said, "D-Money, you couldn't deny him if you wanted to."

"I know right. Good thang, I didn't want to." DeJuan said, walking past Smoke and James to give them dap. They were finishing up what they did best, cutting hair.

Smoke handed his client a mirror and spun him around so that he could see his flawless bald fade. "D-Money, I'ma line Freddy up, then I gotcha, fam."

"I ain't in no rush, bruh. I gotta wait on Chelle to come get Lil D before I can make a move. Plus, I'm waitin on RahRah. Have you seen'em today?" DeJuan asked, grabbing his phone from his back pocket and taking a seat.

"Yeah… you jus missed him. I think he jus goin down to Mr. Johnson's to play his ticket. He said he'd be right back."

"Dat's what's up. And you got me on deck, right?" DeJuan said, speaking of the four and a half ounces of cocaine that he'd been buying from him at least twice a week for the last six months.

"Of course, D-Money."

"Cool."

DeJuan tilted his head back and got lost in a daze, thinking about where he'd come from, where he was, and where he wanted to be.

DeJuan's daily routine had gotten old, and he'd wondered when things would get better. His situation wasn't bad, but at the rate he was moving, it could get ugly real quick. Sitting in the barbershop on 28th and Clifton, he thought about the $11,500 he had in his safe, in his bedroom closet. He knew it wasn't enough to take care of TyChelle and Lil D, and his big break was starting to feel like wishful thinking.

What he was doing now easily brought in five digits a week. But with rent, bills, and luxury expenses for him and his little family, there was no way he could even think about stopping. Lately, what had been heavy on his mind most was figuring out what he needed to do in order for him to be able to stop.

To DeJuan, the hustle wasn't exciting anymore. He felt that the odds were no longer in his favor. He was about to turn twenty-one years old and had done everything that he could imagine when it came to the streets. He knew he could be doing more with his days than hanging around North Nashville waiting on his first case or waiting for someone to try to rob him for the few dollars he was making.

Everyone knew his name. He could always be found in one of three places: the barbershop on 28th, on Andrew Jackson over Talley's house, or on Jefferson Street at the sports bar.

All in all, he had grown tired of those places, tired of the things that brought him there, and was simply looking for more.

Chapter 2
Getting to tha Money

A couple of days later, DeJuan cranked up his engine and was about to put in his favorite Lil Boosie CD when his phone started to vibrate. He looked down, saw Tonya's name and sent her straight to voicemail for the third time that morning. Then he called his homeboy, J-Smooth.

"Wat up, bruh?" J-Smooth answered.

"I'm 'bout to come through… you rollin?" DeJuan asked.

"Yeah, nigga. Come on," J-Smooth said before his feet hit the floor, or even reaching for the pack of Newport's on the night table. "Call me when you outside."

"Aight… and breakfast on you today. Don't forget," DeJuan added before hanging up and pulling off.

As he turned onto Main Street, DeJuan finally decided to answer Tonya's call since she had continued to blow him up.

"Wat's up, Tonya? Yo dude couldn't be around, tha way you dancing on a nigga line… wat's good?"

"If you'd quit playin, you wouldn't have to worry 'bout my man," she started to say, but DeJuan cut her off.

"I'm not worried 'bout dat nigga, and we both know this, but wat's tha deal? You dun called me six times this morning and it ain't even ten o'clock."

"Fuck you, nigga! I just need to get straight. I'm out," she said, referring to the weed that DeJuan supplied her with.

Tonya kept the real reason she'd been calling him the way she was to herself; the gunshots that had woken her up the night before. She had never stopped worrying about DeJuan, especially knowing how he moved in the streets. She knew that moving the way he did attracted plenty of haters.

Although Tonya was mad at that moment, she was also relieved. Mad because DeJuan couldn't see or at least acted as if he didn't know about her feelings for him, but relieved that he was cool and nothing had happened to him.

"Aight girl, I'll be through after I grab something to eat. I'ma hit you when I get to Talley's," DeJuan said.

With the weight lifted from her chest, Tonya said, "Aight nigga," and ended the call.

DeJuan pulled up in front of J-Smooth's crib on the east side, in a neighborhood known as The Bottom. J-Smooth stayed in a two-bedroom Section 8 apartment with his mother. He wasn't there because he couldn't afford to get his own spot, or pay his own way, but because of the relationship he had with his mother.

J-Smooth was an only child, and his father had died in a car wreck when he was thirteen years old. That was the only reason they were on Section 8. When his father passed, he told himself he would always make sure his mother was straight. The only way he felt he could stay true to his word was by sticking around until he saved up enough to buy her a house.

DeJuan blew his horn and waited a couple of minutes. He was about to hit it again when J-Smooth came out looking "dope-boy" fresh. He wore black and gray Trukfit cargo shorts, a black and white Jordan tank top, and white and black retro 11s. His hair was cut in a mohawk, and his 10k pullout grill was flashy, and the 24k gold link chain hanging from his neck shined like the sun. If the saying is true that every tattoo has a story, then his body was a library.

J-Smooth got into the car with DeJuan, they looked like Frick and Frack.

DeJuan had a closet full of Jordans, Air Max's, Air Force 1s, Reebok's, Adidas, and more, but today he had on a pair of brown, navy blue, and cream Perry Ellis deck shoes with khaki Nautica shorts and a navy blue, brown, and cream striped Nautica shirt. A khaki Nautica cap sat on top of his low-cut fade, and a gold watch with a brown leather band wrapped his wrist.

J-Smooth stared at his friend as they headed to the north side of town.

After a few minutes, knowing that DeJuan was purposely ignoring him, J-Smooth said, "Wat up Tiger… I didn't know tha PGA started today, but good luck buddy."

They both busted out laughing.

"Fuck wat you think nigga," DaJuan shot back. "I bet if you had a bitch, she'd like it. Hell, this wat money look like! Now, wat we eating?"

"Yea, wateva… go to IHOP. Monica should be workin dis morning," J-Smooth said.

Once they made it to the restaurant, they were waiting to be seated and saw Monica coming from the back, holding up one finger to signal she'd be just a minute. She knew they would request her as their waitress anyway.

Monica reminded you of Kelly Rowland. She was slim, about 5'9", Hershey-chocolate complexion, full lips and breasts, and a butt that would make any pair of jeans look good. She had long, curly hair that was shiny and black as coal. She had first met DeJuan and J-Smooth the week she started, after they came in high one morning and were seated in her section.

Initially, she thought they were going to give her a hard time, but they actually made that morning a very pleasant one for her. They weren't very demanding, and she liked their vibe. And the two twenty-dollar bills they left as a tip didn't hurt either, seeing that she was going to Vanderbilt on a scholarship.

Before they walked out the door that first day, J-Smooth had her number. Although she was digging DeJuan's swag a little more, she figured that they were both nice and cute. Plus, she hadn't been in a relationship, or anything close to it, since she'd left her hometown, South Carolina, months prior.

She and J-Smooth had been seeing a lot of each other the last few months, but neither one of them were in a rush to put a title on what it was they were doing.

Now, leading them to their table, Monica said, "D-Money, I like those shoes. I didn't know they had Perry Ellis in Sport Seasons."

"These were a gift, but don't get it twisted, I do shop around," he said, taking his seat.

Looking J-Smooth from head to toe, she added, "Well, can you take him with you next time? He always looking thugged out, like he straight out of a drug house."

She saw them exchange a look that made her question, "What's that about?"

"I was just tellin this ni…" DeJuan started, but J-Smooth cut him off.

"Yea, we been through dat already dis morning, and if dis fool wanna run 'round town lookin like Carlton, dat's on him. I ain't no banker or stockbroker, or none of dat shit. I am wat I am," he said, as he slid into the booth with his back to the window and his Jordans on the padded bench.

This time, Monica and DeJuan passed each other a look, and she shook her head before speaking. "Really Smooth? Lemme go get y'all's coffee. We'll finish this later." She turned and went to check on a couple sitting a few tables up from them to take their order, then headed to the back.

Once Monica brought their coffee to the table and took their orders, she strolled off once more, leaving them alone to talk.

They discussed business that had been unattended to while DeJuan had been lost in his thoughts over the last couple of days. It was clearly time to get back to the money. Even though DeJuan was tired of selling drugs, this was his only route to making a living. *It was just too easy,* he thought, as J-Smooth sat across from him, counting money, lining the bills up in stacks of five hundred dollars each.

J-Smooth stopped stacking after the sixth stack and pushed the money towards DeJuan. "Dat's you, bruh. I got dis and 'bout half a P left," he said, holding seventeen hundred in his hand. "But I ain't got no soft. When you gon try to get straight? You know a lot of my people don't want tha tree if it don't come wit tha snow. After I sold K.D. my last two grams and a lil zip, I had to start tellin niggas that I was outta sugar, and dat slowed my shit up like a yellow light."

While talking to DeJuan, J-Smooth looked up and noticed Monica staring at him from the other side of the restaurant, shaking her head. It wasn't that Monica was against hustling, the streets, or the guys in the streets. It was just the ones in the streets that didn't seem to have any ambitions to get out of the streets that got under her skin. She knew that J-Smooth wasn't a bad guy, but she saw that he was complacent.

Approaching with their food, and a little annoyed, Monica said, "Boy! Get that shit off the table," as she set their plates down.

Picking up on her vibe, J-Smooth responded to her energy, saying, "Damn, my gurl… wat's tha matter?"

"Nothing, James. I'm cool," she said, before turning to leave them to their breakfast.

About half an hour later, DeJuan and J-Smooth headed out, leaving Monica a couple of twenties on the table, even though she didn't seem as pleasant as usual. She didn't even check on them anymore that morning.

Once they made it to the car, J-Smooth sent her a text: *CALL ME WEN U GET TIME.*

DeJuan was on his phone making plans to meet up with Smoke and RahRah.

DeJuan never pretended to be the guy who didn't dibble and dabble, but trying to maintain a side chick or any other gal besides TyChelle wasn't worth his trouble. He had too much time invested in his baby momma to mess things up.

TyChelle and DeJuan met in their freshman year at Pearl Cohn High School. They both were in the popular crowd because of who they were or what they had, so it didn't take long for them to meet.

TyChelle Woods was Tyson Wood's daughter. He was one of Nashville's biggest and most publicly known drug dealers. He was charged, convicted, and sentenced to 240 months in federal prison the summer before her freshman year.

She never wanted for anything or had to do too much for herself. The two things she did want were given to her by the feds when she had to go stay with her aunt on 28th Avenue North. Responsibility and freedom. The two things she never expected to experience until well past her 18th birthday were dropped on her like a bomb. TyChelle eagerly accepted the two, as if she had really been listening to her father all those nights when he would talk to her about life until she fell asleep.

Her mother didn't make it through delivery with TyChelle and never got the chance to even see her own little bundle of joy. This, of course, left her father to raise her singlehandedly. Tyson did everything in his power to make sure she'd be straight financially before the feds picked him apart.

There was always the $100,000 he kept at his sister's house, which he knew was safe because she had been an RN at Saint Thomas Hospital since before TyChelle was born. Tyson's sister also owned the two-story, four-bedroom, two-and-a-half-bath home she lived in. Then there was the money from the malpractice lawsuit, which he made sure TyChelle couldn't touch until she was twenty-five years old. He had that stipulation set that way, figuring that if he didn't outlast the game, she'd be straight when the time came.

Tyson also factored in the fact that if and when she emptied the two bank accounts that he had personally set up for her, she would either have a grip on the things she needed and wanted or, more importantly, have learned to be more financially responsible. TyChelle would have access to one bank account at eighteen years old and another at twenty-one. The first held $50,000, and the second held $100,000. Even those amounts would be like raindrops in a bucket compared to the $1.3 million that would be waiting for her when she hit the quarter-century mark from the malpractice suit.

DeJuan Williams' popularity came about a little differently. He pretty much had what he wanted as well.

From the age of ten, he figured out that instead of taking out everybody's trash, on the block every day for one week's worth of lunch money, he could make one trip from Mr. Johnson's house to the store for five times that amount. Once the money started coming in at a steady pace, DeJuan kept a pocket full of cash, and that's when and why he went from being called Dee-Dee to D-Money.

Growing up, DeJuan lived with his grandmother on Herman Street between 24th and 25th Avenue North but was known all over the north side. His mother was wrapped up in a continuing fight and losing battle with her old friend and worst enemy, Mr. Heroin. She did as much as that silver pack allowed her to do, which wasn't much outside of telling him to stay in school and that she loved him, which he truly believed. But as quickly as the words left her mouth, she was out the door again, and it would always be a week or so before she resurfaced. That was something his father never did. What DeJuan knew of his father, he learned from stories told by his aunts, uncles, and grandmother.

DeJuan never really paid too much attention to the stories about his dad. The only thing that mattered to him was having a cute girlfriend, fresh clothes, and money in his pockets. Once he had accumulated the money, the girls came more easily than the clothes. Out of all the girls he had to choose from, it was TyChelle he knew he had to have from the day he laid eyes on her. She had the cutest little heart-shaped face that he'd ever seen, with slanted hazel-brown eyes and a smile that never quit. She was slightly bowlegged, but you couldn't tell until she walked. At 5'3" and 113 pounds, she was a little bitty something.

By this time, DeJuan had formed a habit of getting what he wanted, and when it came to TyChelle, things were no different. At school, they were like Jay-Z and Beyonce` until he got put out in the eleventh grade for having some weed and a gun in his locker. Coincidentally, that was the same year she got pregnant and gave birth to their son, Lil D.

Lil D came a few weeks early on July 31st, but after the doctors let her know that everything was good with their son, she realized that he had come right on time. She was able to start her senior year with her friends and classmates.

TyChelle knew how important it was to her father that she finish school, and it made her proud to do so. Having DeJuan around to watch Lil D so she could finish on time made her even more proud. Their relationship hadn't always been perfect, but it was always solid, leaving no doubt in either of their minds that they would always be able to depend on each other.

Chapter 3
Tha Shop is Hot!

After getting back into the groove of things the day before, DeJuan got up and hit the block earlier than usual the following morning. He was clearly on a money-making mission, determined to dump the rest of the weed he had so RahRah could meet him at the barbershop later to re-up on both the weed and cocaine. DeJuan had given Talley his last twenty-one grams of coke. Talley was an old head who DeJuan looked at like an uncle. His house was where DeJuan spent most of his time when he wasn't at the barbershop.

Freddy entered the barbershop sweating hard with his dreads swinging, as he looked over his shoulders like someone was following him.

"Man… what you done done now!" Smoke said, noticing the paranoid look on Freddy's face.

"Naw, cuz. It ain't me, but dem boys rollin hard 'round dis bitch, and it's an unmarked sittin cross da street," Freddy said.

James, the owner of the shop, went to check on what Freddy had said and saw the navy-blue Impala sitting exactly where Freddy said it was. James shot Smoke a look, letting him know to cease any illegal transactions and to remove any drugs from his shop. He knew full well what Smoke did from behind the barber's chair and didn't want to jeopardize his shop or his freedom. James knew when to put his foot down for the best interest of his business.

Metro had been patrolling the area a little more than everyone was used to, but they didn't seem to have their sights set on anyone in particular. The rookie cops on duty had simply received orders to stay in the vicinity of the store, the restaurant, the gas station, and the plaza where the barbershop was located. These four spots were all located at 28th and Clifton, sitting on the four corners of the intersection adjacent to one another.

With summertime came summer crime, and Metro was just trying to stay ahead of it or at least be prepared for the kind of criminal activities the neighborhood had been known for in the past.

RahRah pulled into the parking lot just as Smoke was headed to his truck to put up his money and little smoke sack, along with the four and a half ounces he had for DeJuan and the 9mm he kept on him at all times.

"Wat up, Smoke?" he said as he got out of his car and headed over to Smoke's Chevy Avalanche.

"Not shit, homie. I thought you was dem people tha way you crept up on tha lot," Smoke said, securing his stash spot by hitting the unlock button twice before turning the key backwards in the ignition.

RahRah almost choked on the blunt he was smoking when he heard that. "I know you lyin nigga."

"Naw, forreal… dey been out dis bitch like tha sun and tha moon for tha last couple days, all day and night. Shid, dey sittin cross tha street now," Smoke said, nodding in the direction of the unmarked.

Peeping the unmarked car through the lenses of his Ray-Bans, RahRah said, "Damn… have D-Money been through today?" He stomped out the butt of the blunt that he dropped.

"Naw, but he posed to be sliding through. I talked to him a lil while ago," Smoke said as they went back into the barbershop.

"Yeah? Bruh told me to be down here at eleven o'clock, it's eleven forty-five," RahRah said, checking the time on his phone. He thumbed through his recent calls to find DeJuan's number.

"Wat's poppin, Rah?" DeJuan said into his phone as he sat at a stoplight on the other side of town.

"I'm at da shop, cuz. Wea you at?"

"I'm 'bout ten minutes out."

"Aight, homie… I'ma chill for a minute, but it's warm out here and I ain't tryna get burnt," RahRah said, referring to the police in the hood.

When DeJuan got off the interstate on 28th and headed in the direction of the barbershop, he passed three unmarked cars and two blue-and-whites before he even made it to Clifton Street. He didn't have anything on him but money, so they didn't worry him. Still, after thinking about it, he figured it would be best to stay at the shop until Metro changed shifts before leaving with the package he was picking up.

"I see those bitches ain't playin today," he said, as he stepped into the shop.

"Hell naw! They got it like a sauna out dis muthafucka, D-Money… had a nigga spooked when I first hit tha block," Freddy said from the chair where James was lining him up.

James laughed and had to stop what he was doing as he pictured Freddy coming through the door again. "D-Money, you shoulda seen'em… he came in here like he was on that shit y'all be sellin, lookin all ova his shoulder like somebody was after him," he said, still laughing.

"Not hard-ass Freddy G!" DeJuan said jokingly.

"Yeah, dat nigga was shakin in dem Chuck Taylors and them hoes ain't cooled down one bit since they started rollin," Smoke said. "But they can't stop a nigga flow. Ya feel me. Wat 'bout you, D-Money?"

"Shid, I gotta job to do, just like them and they ain't tha ones that pay me, so fuck'em! I gotta get to tha money. I gotta family to feed. Plus, I'm tryna have my car painted before my birthday. Aww shit! Y'all gotta come out and fuck wit me. Chelle doin it big for a nigga this year. She throwin me a big bash at Club Agenda, and she got somebody posed to be comin to bring tha city out. I should have some V.I.P. passes in a week or so. I'll come through wit'em if y'all wanna get one," DeJuan said to the whole shop.

"Nigga, you know I want mine homie," Smoke said as he handed an older man a mirror to check out his fade.

"Yeah, bring me one too. You know I gotta come out and kick it wit you for your birthday D-Money," James said.

"Wat 'bout you, Faye?" DeJuan asked.

"Boy, you know I want one, but how much you gon charge me for five of them? I might be able to make my money back off them thangs. I know er'body gon be tryna get in that thang when they find out 'bout it," she said.

"Yeah, I know you ain't gon let a chance to make a hustle pass you up. It just wouldn't be you. I'll give you five for two hundred dollas. Dat way you can let'em fly for fifty a piece and yours'll be free," DeJuan told her.

"Aw hell yeah, D-Money… do that. If I ain't here whenever you come through wit'em, just leave'em wit Smoke or James," Faye said, going into her Coach bag to get the money to pay him.

DeJuan stayed at the barbershop a few more hours, playing dominoes and watching SportsCenter until it was time for Metro to change shifts. That's when he got his sack from Smoke, jumped back in his car, and sped off.

Chapter 4
DeJuan ain't tha Only One Making Moves

TyChelle never lacked playing her part when it came to helping her man stack paper. She had taken on the role of a dope boy's girlfriend and proved to be far more than a kingpin's daughter. In the end, she knew that it would benefit her and her son to do all that she could to make sure things were in order and that DeJuan was stress-free and never rushed or pressed beyond his means.

Therefore, TyChelle had no problem doing things like breaking down weed from pounds to ounces, bagging up cocaine in quarters, halves, and ounces, or even making drop-offs when DeJuan needed her to. She even had a couple of people who would call her two or three times a week to purchase weed directly from her.

One of those sales was the neighbor, Tara, who did hair and sold weed to the majority of the women whose hair she did. Then there was her homegirl, Crissy, who stayed in the projects and went through at least half a pound a week in nickels and dimes.

Selling weed they got from TyChelle and DeJuan wasn't the only thing that Tara and Crissy had in common. They both had growing cocaine habits that started after being introduced to the white powder by HP. HP was a quiet, small-time hustler from the hood who had fathered a child by both Crissy and Tara.

Although HP was small-time, he was still in the streets tough, getting it however it came. This meant he didn't spend a lot of time trying to be America's number one dad. Luckily, the kids had grandmothers who were more than willing to step up. HP's mother kept Tara's little girl, for the most part, and Crissy's mother kept her little girl.

Crissy was waiting for TyChelle to come through and drop off another four ounces of weed, but TyChelle had her on hold waiting on DeJuan. She was wondering what was taking him so long to get back. She placed an order for a large pepperoni and ham pizza, his favorite, and a medium cheese pizza with some hot wings. She told herself that if the pizza got there before DeJuan did, she would just improvise by getting Tara to keep an eye on Lil D until his daddy got home.

Hanging up with Papa John's, TyChelle thought about something she'd heard her father say a thousand times: *"Time wasted is money lost."*

DeJuan was supposed to be coming home so she could make a few runs. Plus, he had said that he needed to use the stove to cook up some cocaine, which was why she was ordering pizza instead of throwing something in the oven or frying some burgers. Knowing that he wanted to cook up, TyChelle figured that he really was on the way, unlike other times when he had said the same thing.

Whether DeJuan made it home or not, TyChelle felt she had things to take care of that were just as important to her as whatever he had going on for himself. Pushing the thoughts of what those things were aside, she started getting herself together. She laid out some jeans and a white and purple Nike T-shirt to go with her purple and white '97 Air Maxes. All TyChelle needed to do now was hop in the shower.

Before doing so, she sat at the foot of the bed, took a deep breath, and leaned back for a moment to relax.

A few minutes later, TyChelle was standing underneath the water in the shower of the bathroom she shared with DeJuan. When she was done, she stepped out of the shower, dried off, and slipped on the purple Victoria's Secret panty and bra set that DeJuan had gotten her earlier that week. She heard the doorbell ring.

She quickly jumped into her jeans and pulled her T-shirt over her head. She headed to the door barefoot, with a twenty and ten in her hand for the pizza and wings.

Lil D was right on her heels once she passed his bedroom, where she had told him to stay and play the game until the pizza arrived. Feeling her son's presence as she paid for the food, TyChelle smiled, knowing he was always hungry and ready to devour whatever she placed in front of him.

After closing the door and turning around, she almost tripped over Lil D as he said, "Momma, I want two big pieces," while she was trying to step around him to get to the kitchen.

"Okay, but you betta eat both of'em," she said, knowing there was probably nothing she would deny him if he asked.

Once she fed Lil D, TyChelle headed back to her bedroom. She grabbed her phone off the dresser and disappeared into the master bathroom, where she simultaneously worked the hair dryer and her phone at the same time. While straightening her hair, she sent out texts to Crissy and DeJuan.

The text to Crissy said, *otw*.

The one she sent to DeJuan read, *if it ain't sumn it's sumn else… WYA… call Tara and check on your son if u can. I gotta take care of sumn like I told u earlie.*

Crissy replied back by the time TyChelle finished in the bathroom, with a simple, *k.*

DeJuan, however, hadn't responded. He knew TyChelle was most likely pissed off at him and wouldn't care to hear any excuses he had about why he still hadn't made it home. The fact that he wasn't even on the way yet wasn't something he thought she'd be trying to hear either. So he decided he would deal with the situation later.

As TyChelle ran bath water for Lil D, she picked up her phone and commanded it to call Tara. She saw her pulling in when she answered the door for the pizza man.

Tara was cool as a fan on high and would do just about anything TyChelle and DeJuan needed her to do. That was mainly because she wanted nothing more than to be just like TyChelle. It didn't hurt that DeJuan kept her supplied with a little personal pack of weed and cocaine to help her get through times when she didn't have or want to spend any extra money.

Tara always kept her appearance up, and from the outside looking in, it seemed like she didn't have a problem in the world. However, HP knew better than anyone. He tried to keep her satisfied by supplying her with cocaine as best he could. He didn't want her out on the streets trying to find it herself. He felt that was the least he could do, seeing that he was the reason she had the habit in the first place.

Chapter 5
Er'body Gotta Play They Part

DeJuan was sitting at the table in Talley's kitchen, breaking down, bagging up, and trying to roll up some weed he had just gotten from RahRah. At the same time, Talley was doing two of the things he did best. The first was talking shit, and he was doing a whole lot of that while cooking up some dope, which was the second of the two.

DeJuan liked to cook his own cocaine and hadn't bought any crack in more than five years. He preferred to turn his cocaine into crack himself, but being that Talley had been the one to put him on game and showed him how to add baking soda to the cocaine and turn one ounce into two, or two into four, DeJuan let him do his thing sometimes.

Not only did he learn the game of "overs" with baking soda from Talley, he also learned how to make real crack with ammonia from him. That was a sure way to keep his phone battery low from all the customers calling trying to get what he had.

Whenever DeJuan had something else to do or was just tired, he would let Talley cook for him. At the moment, he was more than a little occupied. He had three people waiting for a quarter pound each. On top of that, he still had his two main workers to satisfy, Tonya and Lil Mike, who both got a pound each, every time he got straight.

Tonya stayed next door to Talley. She sold her whole pound in grams, easily doubling the $1,050 that DeJuan charged her for it. He didn't know what she was doing with her profit. He figured it must be going to her baby daddy, Cherokee, because she was going through a couple of pounds a week.

Not that it was any of his business, but there was no way for him not to know what he had given her over the last few months, and he saw nothing that resembled progress.

The girl still hadn't even gotten a car, which was supposedly the reason she wanted to sell weed when she first asked DeJuan for a sack. She didn't have a job, but living in the projects meant she didn't really have bills either.

Whatever she had going on, DeJuan didn't allow it to sidetrack him. Other than the couple of times that Tonya was twenty or thirty dollars short, she was always on point. Plus, she had special ways to make up for the difference when she was short.

Lil Mike, on the other hand, took to hustling like a shark to water. He was Talley's nephew, the son of his twin sister. Lil Mike's mother had been killed by a trick when he was seven years old, and he had been living with Talley ever since. He reminded DeJuan of himself.

DeJuan had tried to start him out with just two ounces, but he quickly realized that by doing that, he was asking for a headache. Lil Mike was blowing his phone up three or four times a day. From that point on, DeJuan made sure to hit him off good. He also made sure to drop a few jewels, schooling him in certain areas to ensure he wasn't out there wasting his time.

DeJuan had all the weed separated and bagged up to his approval. Sitting back in a chair, leaning on two legs, he hit the blunt he had just rolled and inhaled deeply.

When Talley yelled, "GODAMNIT!" he spooked DeJuan, almost causing him to fall.

"Wat nigga?" DeJuan said through coughs from the weed smoke caught in his lungs.

"Betty Crocker, da Girl Scouts or dat Pilsbury mutha-fucka couldn't show you a cookie dat look dis fuckin good nigga!" Talley said, turning the Pyrex jar upside down, letting the cocaine, which was now a solid slab of crack, slowly slide out of the jar onto the counter.

To neither of their surprise, when the finished product hit the counter, not a crumb broke off. It was solid as a rock and sure to satisfy the crack fiends that came to Talley's, looking for the high-quality drugs he was known to keep.

The few dudes who copped quarters and half ounces from DeJuan did so because they knew he kept the best dope around.

DeJuan held the finished product in one hand and hit the blunt with the other. He nodded in approval and prepared to place the dope on the scale that Talley had gotten out of the cabinet.

"Not half bad," he said. "I gotta admit, when it comes to burnin, you always have been pretty fair for a square."

"Until you get some of dis shit, dat comes in squares, wrapped and stamped, you ain't talkin 'bout a bitch-ass thang, young nigga... I been doin dis shit," Talley said after picking up and hitting a blunt roach that DeJuan had left in the ashtray.

DeJuan cracked up laughing. He loved hearing Talley talk shit and always knew what to say or do to get him started.

Seeing that DeJuan was just getting a laugh out of him, Talley said, "Fuck you nigga. Gimme a gram of dat powder before you drop it all. I'm finna go see wat tha block doin."

Seeing that the ounce Talley cooked up had jumped to thirty-one grams, DeJuan said, "Take two and anotha one hard while you're at it. Spread it out a lil bit so we can hurry up and get this shit gone."

Talley did what DeJuan said and headed out the front door.

DeJuan cooked up two more ounces and kept the rest for powder sales. By the time Talley made it back, DeJuan was sitting at the table, enjoying the last of another blunt and thinking about the profit he was about to make from what was in front of him.

With the extra grams that he got from the cook-up, DeJuan was looking at a free quarter ounce. Add that to the three ounces of hard and forty grams of soft, include the ten pounds of weed that was also on the table, and he calculated a total of $18,600 coming back to him within a couple of days. That meant a profit of $9,500 that he was looking at. $5,500 from the weed and another $4,000 coming from the work.

DeJuan couldn't wait until he found someone to sell him cocaine cheaper, but he knew all too well not to rush it. The $9,000 to $10,000 he was pulling in two, maybe three, times a week was doing more than paying his bills, so he wasn't about to complain.

The sound of his phone vibrating on the table pulled him out of the daze he had slipped into. When he saw Tonya's name on the screen, he answered. "I gotcha on deck my girl. Wat you want me to do, cause I was 'bout to start movin 'round?"

"You can just leave it at Talley's. I'll get it," she said. "But can I meet you a lil later and pay you cause I need to talk to you 'bout something... and it's important?"

Looking at his G-Shock to check the time, he said, "Wat is it? You might as well holla at me now."

"What? You gon be too busy for me to get atchu later?" she teased. "You know there's a time and place for everything, and now ain't tha time, and Talley's definitely ain't tha place for what I want to talk to you about, but if you gon be busy, I understand." Her voice carried a combination of seduction and disappointment.

DeJuan thought he knew what she wanted and figured he'd take her up on it if he was right. "Aight, Tonya, meet me ova my nigga Smooth spot 'bout eight, nine o'clock. I'll shoot you a text to let you know when I'm there," he said.

"Cool," she replied before they both hung up.

DeJuan needed to hook up with J-Smooth later to give him an ounce of powder and a few pounds of weed anyway, so he figured he could kill two birds at once. He called his partner and got him on the line.

"Wat up, nigga," J-Smooth answered, seeing that it was DeJuan.

"Bruh, I'ma be swangin your way 'bout eight. I got yo bag. Plus, Tonya need to holla at me. I told her to meet me there… dat cool?" DeJuan stated, letting him know the business.

"You know it's straight nigga. Jus let me know when you on tha way so I can look out for you."

"Aight fam… I'ma hit you up later then," DeJuan said and ended the call.

"Wat up big homie?" Lil Mike said as he walked in through the back door and saw DeJuan sitting at the table.

"Jus workin, Magic Mike," DeJuan replied, calling him by the nickname he had given him when he first saw how fast he got rid of the weed that he supplied him with. He had told him back then that he had to be a magician the way he was making the weed disappear.

Lil Mike accepted the nickname but corrected DeJuan. He let him know that he wasn't simply making the weed disappear; he was turning it into stacks of bills.

That answer alone let DeJuan know that Lil Mike respected the game that he was playing and had what it took to become a major player.

Lil Mike didn't carry himself the way a lot of the dudes his age that called themselves hustlers did. Most of them stayed in the latest fashion and trending clothing. Lil Mike was cool in a plain white, black, or gray T-shirt with sweatpants or jeans. The one thing he did keep was a fresh pair of kicks on his feet, and his dreads looked like they had just been retwisted every time you saw him.

Where those other dudes kept a wad of money on them at all times, some even had all of their money on them, Lil Mike made a trip to the house every time he made a hundred dollars to put it up. The other guys wanted to be seen and heard. Lil Mike just wanted to get paid. DeJuan liked this about him.

DeJuan started gathering his things to head out as Lil Mike poured himself a glass of Kool-Aid. As he placed the pitcher back in the refrigerator, he heard DeJuan say, "I was gon leave dis wit yo uncle, but since you're here… here."

DeJuan tossed him a pound in a Ziplock bag. "And let Talley know I put dis up here," he added, placing twenty-eight grams in the cabinet where they kept the scales, baking soda, and anything else they needed for their line of work.

After that, DeJuan grabbed his Nike backpack with the rest of the weed and coke inside, threw it over his shoulder, and picked up his phone.

The phone went from the table to the clip on his belt just as his right hand went to the Glock 9 tucked in his waistband. With this final security measure, he was out the front door.

Chapter 6
Doin Too Much

DeJuan went to the house to put up the excess weed and money he had on him. He knew he wasn't going to need it for the rest of the night. With that small chore taken care of, he headed back towards the door.

TyChelle was lying back on the loveseat watching Love and Hip-Hop and said, "Where you goin wit yo sneaky ass?"

"Ova J-Smooth's. I gotta take'em this," DeJuan said, showing her the weed and coke he had for J-Smooth. "Plus tha game 'bout to come on. So we might go to tha sports bar for a few. Why? Wat's up?"

"Nun," she said, throwing her hand up, waving him off.

What TyChelle hated more than anything was going to bed alone. With DeJuan leaving that late in the day, it was a good indication she would be closing out the night alone.

"Aight… well, call me if you think you might need me before I get back, or think of something you might want me to pick up while I'm out," DeJuan said as he headed out the door.

He sent a text to Tonya from his driveway before pulling off.

Before making it to J-Smooth's house, DeJuan stopped by the store and the liquor store. He needed Swishers and knew how Tonya liked her Peach Amsterdam.

As he pulled onto J-Smooths' street, he saw Tonya sitting in her homegirl's truck and pulled up beside her. The windows were rolled up, and he could barely see through the tint.

When he stepped out of his car, she cracked the window. "So wat now Dee?"

"Just chill. Let me holla at my nigga real quick," he said. "You in a rush or something? You on some type of time frame? Let me know cause I ain't tryna get you in trouble." He handed her the bottle and cigars. "I'll be right back."

He walked off in the direction of J-Smooth's front porch.

Knowing DeJuan was on the way, J-Smooth already had the door cracked. He had heard the pipes on DeJuan's Monte Carlo when he turned onto the street.

"Man, Chelle gon kill tha both of y'all if she eva find out you still been fuckin wit Tonya afta all dis time," J-Smooth said as DeJuan walked into the kitchen.

"I know, right," DeJuan said, moving around the kitchen like it was his. He grabbed two plastic cups and filled them with ice from the trays in the freezer. "That's why I need you to do me a favor tonight." He set the cups down and pulled the weed and cocaine from his waistband, where he had tucked it before getting out of the car, and handed it to J-Smooth.

"Yea, wats dat?" J-Smooth said, opening the Ziplock bag and sticking his nose in it.

"Take my car and go to tha sports bar for a lil while. If anybody come looking for me, or ask 'bout my whereabouts, jus tell'em I went to catch a play and I should be right back."

"Yeah, I gotcha," J-Smooth said, knowing that he could easily make him a few hundred dollars while he was there.

"Cool… I'm finna hop in tha truck wit Tonya. I'll hit you up if I need you." DeJuan grabbed the cups and headed outside.

He got into the truck, placed the cups of ice in the cup holders, and looked over at Tonya. "Wat's up, my girl?"

DeJuan rubbed her thigh while looking into her eyes with the same devilish grin that she had seen numerous times before but never got tired of looking at.

Tonya looked into DeJuan's big brown eyes and immediately got lost in her thoughts. Snapping out of it, she twisted the top off the bottle and poured their drinks. She continued staring at him until he broke her gaze.

"Wat's so important it couldn't wait til tha mornin, Tonya," he said, bringing her back to the here and now.

"You say that like you tired of fuckin wit me or something," she said, pushing what she really wanted to say out of her head.

"Now you know if that was tha case, we wouldn't even be here right now. So come on… think 'bout wat you gon say before you spit that shit out." He replied, taking a drink from his cup.

Caught up in her feelings, Tonya said what she initially wanted to say. "Damn… a bitch miss you and wanna spend a lil time with you," she said, looking straight ahead. "And this what I get?"

"Aww, ain't that sweet. You miss me?" he said, leaning over trying to kiss her on the cheek.

"Fuck you! I don't know why I even bother," she said, blocking his face with her hand.

"Well, you know I ain't got no problem wit you fuckin me," he said, grabbing the cigars and breaking one down. "But I really thought yo nigga had that lil pussy on lock. Shid, you ain't gave me none in a nice lil minute. Wat's that bout?"

"Boy stop, and if he did, you know you got tha master key. You and Chelle just been playin house. Must be nice," she said, watching him roll up.

DeJuan didn't respond. He never talked about TyChelle or their relationship.

"Where we goin, Dee? I know you on tha clock and prolly ain't got too much time," she said, wishing she wasn't right.

"The Marriott. Bellevue. But let's just roll for a second. Hop on tha interstate," he said, putting the blunt in the ashtray and lighting a Newport before taking another swallow from his cup.

Tonya eventually pulled away from in front of J-Smooth's house. They rode around the city sipping and smoking without saying too much until DeJuan turned the radio down, silencing Drake.

"Gon shoot to tha spot before we end up fuckin out here on 65 and gettin arrested for indecent exposure," he said, while rubbing her inner thigh. He traced the lining of her panties then slid a finger up inside of her shorts.

When he felt that she was already wet, he proceeded beyond the lining of her panties, sliding his fingers to where her pussy lips parted and slid, not one, but two fingers inside of her juice box. He played around, sliding his fingers in and out of her until she couldn't take it anymore.

"Stop before you make me wreck," she said.

DeJuan removed his hand from between her thighs and sucked the juices from one of his fingers before sticking the other into her mouth so she could taste herself. With them, everything was a go. There was nothing they hadn't tried when it came to sex. They have been fucking since high school, and regardless of who shared Tonya's bed with her, or what TyChelle thought, they would always be each other's jump-off.

By the time they made it to the hotel, they had almost finished the bottle and were definitely feeling the effects of the alcohol.

Once they were inside the room, Tonya started moving like she had a mission to complete. That mission seemed to be getting DeJuan inside of her.

He was sitting on the side of the bed, about to roll another blunt when she knelt down between his legs and went to work on his zipper.

Once she had him in her hand, Tonya took him into her mouth like a melting popsicle. She licked, slurped, and sucked, but unlike a popsicle, the more she sucked, the bigger he got. It wasn't long before she could no longer fit him completely in her mouth. By then, rolling a blunt was the furthest thing from his mind. Instead, he grabbed her head and guided it up and down as she worked her mouth like a suction cup on his dick.

Tonya removed her hands from his pole, allowing DeJuan to freely fuck her face, knowing that he liked it more when she did it with no hands. As he felt himself about to explode, he pulled out of her mouth. It wasn't because she didn't like him cumming in her mouth, but because she loved it when he nutted on her. The feeling of warm cum on her face, ass, titties, back, or wherever, just about drove her crazy. That feeling alone was enough to bring her to an orgasm.

When DeJuan shot his load on her face, her hand instantly went to work on her own zipper. A split second later, her hand was in her shorts with two fingers inside of her and her thumb working on her clit.

Once DeJuan had fully released himself, he laid back on the bed completely relaxed. His break from ecstasy was short-lived. Tonya peeled off her clothes and began undressing him. After pulling him up to a sitting position so she could get his shirt over his head, she mounted him in the sixty-nine position, all in what seemed like one motion.

While sucking on her pearl tongue, DeJuan was also circling her asshole with his thumb. In response, she circled the head of his dick, bringing it back to full length within a couple of minutes. Even though his mouth made Tonya feel like she was on top of the world, she knew that once he got inside of her and started to touch that spot, one that no one but DeJuan seemed able to touch, she would feel like she was in another world.

The anticipation of that out-of-this-world feeling caused her to switch positions. Rising from his face, Tonya turned and positioned herself so she could slowly slide down onto DeJuan's lovestick. As she did, he began filling her up like no other man ever had.

DeJuan simply leaned back and let Tonya take control. She moved on his pole like she was competing in a hula-hoop contest and didn't want to settle for anything less than first place. She moved her wide hips in a circular motion, sending feelings of ecstasy through DeJuan's entire body, from his head down to his toes.

His body tensed just as Tonya reached her orgasm, spilling her juices all over him. DeJuan grabbed her by the waist and felt her relax in his grip. Pulling her down onto himself a few more times, he thrust his way to another orgasm of his own.

Tonya collapsed on DeJuan's chest, catching her breath. He sat up and automatically reached for his weed and cigars. Tonya already knew their stay wouldn't be a long one, so when DeJuan began rolling up, she headed to the bathroom to shower quickly. Tonya could not, and would not, take the smell of sex home with her.

DeJuan rolled a couple of blunts and smoked half of one before Tonya came out of the bathroom naked, still patting herself dry with the small hotel towel that would never make it around her waist. When she walked past DeJuan, with her ass and perky titties shaking like Jell-O, he playfully smacked her butt, making her smile. She had gotten exactly the reaction she wanted.

After finishing the blunt, DeJuan went into the bathroom to wash off, never giving a second thought as to why he had never left Tonya alone. He knew it was her free spirit, and the bond they shared without any real commitment to one another. That made their escapades that much more enjoyable.

"Come on. I gotta get back to tha hood before I'm missed. And I know yo nigga lookin for you by now." DeJuan said coming out of the bathroom. He grabbed the other blunt from the ashtray and headed towards the door.

"Yeah, well if he is, dat's his problem, cause I'm grown and on my own time and ain't gotta answer to nobody, unlike you," she shot back at him.

DeJuan snickered, "You got dat." He decided to drive because he felt Tonya was closer to crashing than he was. DeJuan grabbed the keys and they headed out.

They had just pulled off the lot and into traffic when Tonya popped open the glove compartment, pulled out a wad of bills, and put them onto DeJuan's lap, brushing against his hardness as she did.

Money had always been DeJuan's number one motivator. So it was only natural that his manhood instinctively came alive at the sight of the fives, tens, and twenties spread across his lap. Even though it was just a little more than a thousand dollars, the sight of it brought out his animal side.

As soon as he turned onto the interstate ramp, he pulled his dick out, grabbed Tonya by the back of the neck, and guided her head downward where she eagerly took him into her mouth. Her lips stayed wrapped around his pole even as they pulled into the alley behind the sports bar where J-Smooth was sitting in his car, waiting.

Before exiting the car, DeJuan parked, then released his load, which Tonya caught and swallowed every drop of. After, he got out of the truck and headed towards his car.

He got in on the passenger side of his whip. J-Smooth immediately put the car in drive and headed home, knowing DeJuan would want to do the same.

About forty-five minutes after leaving the sports bar, DeJuan made it home. He eased into bed with TyChelle after removing Lil D from their bed and taking him to his room.

TyChelle never budged.

Chapter 7
Haters Gon' Hate

It was still early when Freddy turned onto Blank Street from Jackson Street. He was heading to Tonya's to get a sack and see if his cousin, Cherokee, wanted to match a couple of blunts. Just as he reached her porch and was about to knock on the door, he couldn't help but turn around when he heard what sounded like TSU's marching band coming up the street.

"Fuck you! Fuck you!" is what Freddy heard as DeJuan came up from Herman Street, shaking everything with his new system blasting Yo Gotti.

The six twelve-inch JL audio woofers, pushed by a Rockford Fosgate amp, had everybody on the block throwing up their middle fingers and rapping along with the beat. Freddy no longer had to knock on the door. DeJuan had already brought Cherokee and several other people in the hood, outside with the CMG concert he had coming from his trunk.

As Cherokee opened the door for his cousin, he saw that it was DeJuan who had woken him, and anyone else who may have been asleep at that time of the afternoon.

"He need to be gettin a paint job instead of ridin 'round tryna be heard," Cherokee said.

Tonya was upstairs changing out of the sweatpants and T-shirt she had on all morning into some leggings and a halter top. She had seen DeJuan pull up from her bedroom window. She knew she would need to meet him at Talley's to get the weed she had told him she needed and give him the money she owed him from the last pound. Tonya tried to never be caught off her square by anyone, especially DeJuan. With the braids she had spent all morning getting done, she looked like Janet Jackson in Poetic Justice as she ran down the stairs and headed for the door.

"Where tha fuck you goin?" Cherokee yelled from the kitchen with powder on his nose and Freddy's pack in his hand.

Tonya rolled her eyes but quickly wiped the look of disgust off her face before turning around. "I gotta get some weed from D-Money. Then I'm goin to tha mall to get something to wear to tha club next week."

"Who said you could go to tha club?" Cherokee said, laughing as he looked over at Freddy.

"I been grown… one, two, three, uhh five years," she shot back. "So, I didn't ask nobody where I could or couldn't go. Plus, it's my homegirl's birthday."

She lied, hoping it would make things all right in his mind. Her mind was already made up. She knew she was going when DeJuan gave her the V.I.P. pass to his birthday bash. It had been in her panty drawer for three days.

Tonya really didn't want any extra, unnecessary beef, so she left and headed next door to take care of her business with DeJuan.

DeJuan had everything ready for her. Talley handed her a Ziplock bag stuffed full with some of the lightest and fluffiest weed you could find in Nashville. As soon as she was inside Talley's, she exchanged green for green and turned right back towards the door.

Tonya and DeJuan always made sure to keep their business calls, meetings, and their transactions as quick as possible. They didn't want to cause anyone to think they had something going on. The less attention they got, the better.

Before heading out the door, Tonya turned to DeJuan and said, "If you ain't finna be tied up too long and can make time for a bitch, hit me up. I just bought a few hours away from dude."

"I might just have to make time, tha way you lookin right now," DeJuan said, watching her turn to walk out the door.

Back at her place, Tonya put up the weed, gave Freddy the sack he came for, and gave Cherokee the last couple ounces from the last batch of weed she had gotten. Then she picked up the keys to his Tahoe and walked out the door without saying a word.

There wasn't much Cherokee could say since it was Tonya who paid all but two payments of the car notes, and she was the one who bought the twenty-six-inch rims that had him turning heads every time he rolled through the city.

After adjusting the seat and putting in her latest favorite CD, Tonya sat for a second, thinking about how sick and tired she was of making Cherokee look as if he was taking care of business when it was really all her. Without her in the picture, their relationship, or what was left of it, would be worth less than an empty frame.

Why couldn't he be more like DeJuan? she thought before putting the SUV in drive.

Tonya pulled off feeling some type of way, hoping DeJuan decided to make good on his word to call her when he left Talley's.

Inside Tonya's place, Cherokee and Freddy sat at the kitchen table breaking down weed, cocaine, and Swishers.

"I gotta give it to dat weak ass nigga, D-Money, he keep dat kill," Cherokee started. "Why he keep ridin 'round in dat old ass Monte Carlo is jus dumb. But hey, dat's him."

"Yeah, he dun had it for a minute," Freddy said, placing one freshly rolled blunt on the table and reaching for another cigar. "But I think he said something 'bout gettin it sprayed and bringin it out for his birthday. And I can say, dat mutha-fuack runnin like a scared bitch."

"Yeah," Cherokee said, enthusiastically.

"Wat up, you goin to his birthday bash at Agenda?"

"Tha fuck I look like… a D-Money fan? Naw, I ain't goin to dat shit. You know I don't do clubs," Cherokee said, reaching for the blunt.

"Hoe, I was jus askin. Niggas was talkin 'bout it at tha shop like it was gon be lit. If I ain't got nothing else to do, I might slide through and see wat's poppin. I ain't no D-Money fan neither, but if it's gon' be off tha chain like they was sayin, then I know it's gon' be plenty of hoes there. And pussy is one thing I'll always be a fan of. Dat shit runnin neck and neck wit air… I don't know which one is betta. So fuck D-Money! I ain't gon' be checkin for him. I'm goin for tha hoes!" Freddy made it clear.

"My bad, cuz. Well, I guess if I ain't doin shit and it can be beneficial, then fuck it, I'll roll. I know some niggas gon' be in dat bitch stuntin," Cherokee said, trying to plant the seed in his cousin's head for a possible robbery.

Cherokee and Freddy weren't really the hustling type. It wasn't that they didn't know the ins and outs of the dope game and pretty much everybody that played a part in it. No, they just figured it was a waste of time to run around trying to sell drugs when they could just rob someone for their drugs and money and spend their time enjoying the high they got from doing the drugs.

In the streets, they had built a name for themselves as robbers.

Being from the north side, one thing they made sure to do was take their show on the road. The majority of their victims came from other parts of town. They rarely wore masks, and more often than not, they left their victims not just penniless, but also bleeding, if not breathless.

This was the reason Cherokee didn't like to go out to clubs. He never knew who he might run into and couldn't recall everybody he had crossed.

Chapter 8
Never Re-rock

"Gurl, you still hittin tha mall wit me later?" TyChelle asked Crissy over the phone as she fixed Lil D a bowl of Lucky Charms.

"Oow shit… yeah bitch. Wha-at time yoouu going?" Crissy said, her voice breaking through moans of pleasure as her boyfriend, and baby daddy, HP skillfully brought her to the edge of ecstasy.

He applied just enough pressure to her clit with the tip of his tongue, bringing her to the brink of explosion.

"Bitch, y'all don't never stop," TyChelle said. She was referring to how much Crissy and HP had sex. "Call me when you get off his dick," she playfully added before hanging up.

She turned her attention back to Lil D, who was looking up at her with milk running down his chin.

"You wanna go shoppin with your mommy today or hang with your daddy?" she asked Lil D, standing over him with a bowl of Frosted Flakes in her hand.

"I wanna go witchu… you gon buy me sumn?" he said.

"Yea boy. Watchu want?"

"Iono, but when I see it, I'ma show you," he said, looking up at her.

TyChelle just shook her head. "Alright. I got you," she said before finishing her cereal and texting DeJuan to let him know what she had planned for the day.

She was running Lil D's bath water when Crissy called her back an hour later.

"Wat's up slut?" TyChelle answered, jokingly.

"Fuck you hoe… don't get me started on you and D-Money, wit y'all freaky asses," Crissy shot back.

"Aight gurl… I'm sorry, *not*. Let me know when tha baby shower is," TyChelle said and they both started laughing.

"Bitch, wat time you gon' be ready?" Crissy asked.

"I can be ova there in 'bout thirty minutes. I just gotta get Lil D dressed. Really, I been waitin on you and HP to get through gettin it in, or should I say gettin it out".

"Whateva, Chelle, come on. I'll be ready when you get here."

They hung up.

TyChelle dressed Lil D and headed out of the house. Crissy spotted TyChelle coming around the drive from her daughter's window as she finished packing some clothes into a backpack.

She stepped off the porch just as TyChelle came to a stop in front of her.

"I need to take this to my momma's house. Precious stayin wit her for anotha week or two," Crissy said, tossing the backpack into the back seat before playfully smacking Lil D.

"Aight now, don't say nun when I let'em out that car seat and he get on yo ass," TyChelle said.

"Gurl, my boyfriend know I'm just playin. Don't you, Lil D?"

Lil D nodded his head as his mother spoke up, "Wateva. We'll swing by there when we leave Opry Mills. I'm tryna beat tha traffic. Plus, I might mess around and have to go to tha Gucci store in Green Hills anyway."

"Aw shit now! We ballin, ain't we?" Crissy said.

"Naw, hoe, we ain't ballin, but it is DeJuan's birthday. Hell, I can spend a lil sumn on him. He deserves it," TyChelle said.

"I guess… Well, I don't know what I wanna get, but I definitely ain't rockin nothing outta my closet," Crissy said, staring out the window, wondering if she had enough cash for a little red dress and some shoes from the Coach store, thinking about the many Coach bags she already had.

As TyChelle, Crissy, and Lil D moved through the mall, it looked as if they were just collecting bags - Nike, Levi, Ralph Lauren, and more. Crissy had a couple of Coach bags. One bag held a purple and turquoise, low-cut, tight-fitting dress with the back out. The other held a pair of four-inch, strapless turquoise heels.

"Bitch, I'ma kill'em when I get this dress on my fine ass," Crissy said, walking out of the Coach store. "Plus, tha bag I bought last month go right wit it… and my white shades wit tha purple 'C'… yeah, they dead when I step in that piece."

They headed towards the food court.

While standing in line waiting for Lil D's slice of Sbarro's pizza, which he just had to have every time they visit the mall, TyChelle noticed him staring across the food court at some girl waving at him from the Chinese spot. TyChelle observed their interaction.

The girl grabbed her food and headed in their direction. As she got closer, Crissy and TyChelle realized it was their old friend, Shanell.

The three of them were inseparable throughout high school. It was after TyChelle had given birth to Lil D and officially became DeJuan's baby mama that everything changed, and she and Shanell stopped speaking.

TyChelle had known that DeJuan and Shanell had a thing before her, but she felt that Shanell should've respected the relationship. So when she heard that DeJuan had been seen leaving Shanell's house one night after a football game, the next day at school, TyChelle confronted Shanell in the hallway, and Crissy had to get between them to stop them from coming to blows.

As Shanell was approaching, it was like they had all been pulled back to that moment that left Crissy as the middleman.

Neither TyChelle nor Crissy had seen Shanell since graduation, but Crissy and Shanell still kept in touch. Shanell was in her senior year of college and had been staying on campus. Being that she was only forty-five minutes away at Austin Peay, she was in the city every week or so.

Shanell broke the awkward tension, speaking first, "What's happening, Crissy? Hey Chelle."

"Nothing much, girl. Wat you doin here?" Crissy asked.

TyChelle gave her the universal nod and a full once over, silently admitting to herself that Shanell looked damn good.

The short haircut Shanell was rocking was a new look for her. She had always worn her hair long and silky. The jeans she had on, with a Miami Heat Lebron James jersey and black, red, and white retro 8s, looked as if they were painted on to her body.

Shanell had never been the girly-girly type, but no man would ever mistake her for anything less than one hundred percent woman. Whether she was in sweats or a swimsuit, her presence demanded attention of any man in the vicinity.

"Tryna find something for my momma birthday. She'll be the big four-oh next week," Shanell said, feeling the energy that was coming from TyChelle while she continued to stare at her.

Shanell acted as if she didn't notice the way TyChelle had her nose turnt up. She looked at Lil D. "I know this ain't the lil baby that used to cry all the time, looking like a whole little man… what's goin on, lil man? How old are you?"

"I'm four, and my name ain't lil man, it's Lil D," he corrected her.

"Uhh, well I'm sorry, DeJuan Williams Jr.," she said, noticing Lil D's reaction. He squinched his face in confusion looking up at his mother. "Well, I ain't gon hold y'all up. It was good to see y'all. Bye Lil D."

Shanell headed in the direction of Zales.

Lil D didn't say anything, but his eyes followed her until she disappeared into the crowd.

Once she was gone, he patted his mother's leg until she looked down at him. "Who was dat lady? How she know my name?" Lil D asked.

Had things turned out differently, TyChelle's answer would have been different. She probably would have said that Shanell was his godmother or that she was her best friend, which she used to be.

Being that things had changed, her answer was simple. "She's just a girl that went to school with me," TyChelle said dryly and left it at that.

TyChelle, Crissy, and Lil D got their food, sat down, ate, and then left Opry Mills Mall to head to Green Hills Mall. TyChelle was determined to get DeJuan's birthday gift from Gucci, and what she wanted to get for him she didn't see at the outlet mall.

Chapter 9
Tha Cat's Out

DeJuan woke up to the sound of his phone vibrating on the nightstand beside the bed. He rubbed his face with both hands and was stretching when he noticed the time on the clock was almost noon. The clock read eleven-forty-eight. Grabbing his phone, he saw six missed calls and three more notifications. Two missed calls were from J-Smooth. Two were from Talley. Then he had one from Tonya and one from TyChelle.

The last notification was a text from Tonya. He checked it first, being that it was the one that woke him up.

The text read, *I'M PREGNANT.*

The text before that was from J-Smooth and said, *HMU wen u get up.*

Then there was another from Tonya that said, *CAN WE TALK.*

After reading the texts, he called TyChelle, seeing that she was first on his list of priorities.

"Wat's up, bae?" he said when she answered. "I just got up. You good?"

"Yeah. I'm straight, baby. Me and your son had stopped at Waffle House, and after I ordered our food, he said exactly what I was thinking," TyChelle said, leaving DeJuan to wonder what her and Lil D had on their minds.

"And wat was that?"

"His lil smart ass said, '*You know daddy gon be hungry when he get up. Why you ain't get him nothing.*'"

DeJuan laughed. "Well, I'm glad y'all thought about me, but I'm straight. I'll grab me a lil something somewhere, but I'm bull-shittin, I shoulda been up and outta here long time ago." DeJuan got up and moved towards the bathroom.

"Well, take care of your business, baby, and be careful. We'll see you later," TyChelle said before they disconnected.

Now that DeJuan was fully awake, he gave Tonya's texts some real thought. After a moment, he shot her a text back saying, *SMH AGAIN I GUESS U SAYIN ITS MINE...U BET NOT BE PLAYIN ME 4 $... UNO IF I FIND OUT U PLAYIN IMA CUT U OFF.*

After sending the text, he turned on the shower and got ready to hop in. Less than fifteen minutes later, DeJuan was out of the shower, dressed, and out the door.

At Tonya's house, Cherokee was babysitting her phone like it was a winning lottery ticket. He had gone into the bathroom while Tonya was in the shower to take a leak and just happened to see her phone sitting on the back of the toilet, with a text she must have forgotten to send. It was to DeJuan, and even though Cherokee knew they did business together, something about the text felt like more than business.

After pressing send on the, *CAN WE TALK* text, Cherokee's mind went into overdrive. He wondered, *what did they need to talk about.* Then he thought of a better way to get an answer.

He took the phone with him out of the bathroom and waited. When he heard the shower cut off, he thought of a better way to get a response and the answer to the question in his head. He sent another text saying, *I'M PREGNANT.*

He knew whatever response came back would tell it all. Now, he just had to wait for the reply.

Cherokee turned his phone off, plugged it into the charger and yelled to Tonya that he was using hers because his was dead.

She paid no attention to him. Her phone was set up so that her outgoing texts were automatically deleted. Plus, she figured that if DeJuan did respond to the text that she thought she sent, it would just be a simple, *ok* or *'bout wat.*

Regardless, if Cherokee asked any questions, she would fall back on, *it's just business*, as her cover.

DeJuan was on the interstate, heading toward the north side. He had just finished lining things up with J-Smooth when his thoughts drifted back to Tonya and the texts. He knew that a baby would ruin everything that he and TyChelle had going on. Especially a baby by Tonya.

He called Tonya to get to the bottom of it only to get her voicemail. He called back and got her voicemail again, like the phone was turned off, or the battery was dead. He tried one more time and got the same results. He decided to send a text instead, *HOLLA AT ME WEN I GET TO THA HOOD*.

But that didn't work either. His phone beeped, letting him know his text had not been delivered.

DeJuan didn't know what to think, but he couldn't let it get him off course. He continued in the direction of the barbershop, his first stop. He needed to pick up some work from Smoke before heading to Talley's to post up for the day.

The last text DeJuan sent Tonya couldn't have made the situation Tonya was in any better.

When Cherokee read the text, he didn't make it past, *SMH AGAIN*, before he stormed into the bathroom where Tonya was.

She knew from the look in his eyes something was wrong. Before either of them knew what was happening,

Cherokee smacked her across the face with her phone so hard that it fell to the floor in pieces. Then he grabbed her by the throat and started to choke her.

Tonya tried, with all the strength she could muster, to fight Cherokee off, feeling that her life was on the line. She felt his hands tightening around her neck. But she wasn't strong enough to break free. With his grip tightening, she faded in and out of consciousness. By the time she hit the floor, Cherokee was on top of her until she completely passed out and was motionless.

He stripped her naked and raped her repeatedly. Then he tied her up and pushed her to the back of their bedroom closet. After that, Cherokee went straight to her stash.

He took the twelve ounces of weed that were in a knock-off Chanel bag and the $3,200 that was in a jewelry box on the dresser.

Then he started packing his clothes into a couple of duffel bags, taking them out to his truck. A lot of what he was doing was done without any thought at all. He was running through the house like a mini tornado, leaving it in shambles. He was focused on getting out of there with what he thought he deserved.

As Tonya fought to regain consciousness, the only thing she could remember, and kept hearing was Cherokee screaming, *'So you fuckin D-Money BITCH! Huh, HOE... You been givin dat bitch ass NIGGA my pussy!'*

She pushed those thoughts out of her head and focused on freeing her hands and feet. Getting out of the closet was the only thing on her mind. She felt the pain around her ankles and wrist. Tonya didn't know how long she had been in that closet, but she hoped and prayed that Cherokee was nowhere around, if and when she made it out.

While Tonya was at home trying to free herself from restraints, Cherokee sat in his truck at the sports bar with a gram of cocaine broken down in a ten-dollar bill. No matter how many snorts he took, he was still boiling and fucked up mentally about the situation back at Tonya's. He knew something was going on between Tonya and DeJuan, but whenever he said anything about it, she would always use the fact that they were doing business as an excuse.

He was pissed off, and the more powder he put up his nose, the more pissed off he became. After what he did to Tonya, he intended to get enough powder to snort and smoke his problems away.

He was almost finished with the eight ball he had gotten from Rodney, the owner of the sports bar, and Cherokee thought about the immediate and necessary changes he was going to have to make.

One of the first changes would be his living situation. Where was he going to lay his head? How was he going to keep some money flowing? Even though he took Tonya's weed and helped her sell it in the past, her clientele was hers. He didn't have any weed customers of his own. With him being away from her house, it really did no good for him to have the weed, besides the fact that he needed it to put the cocaine on.

Cherokee wasn't so naive as to think twelve ounces would set him straight. The weed and the few thousand dollars would only last for so long. He had to come up with a lucrative plan to bring in some money. It was time to make something shake.

The sun had gone down, and it started to sprinkle. As the raindrops hit the windshield, Cherokee watched the water run down the window. He felt as if he just might drown in the anger and hatred he felt towards Tonya and DeJuan. He rolled another blunt before getting out of the truck to go get a beer from inside the bar. And that's when he thought of the answer to all of his problems.

Cherokee hurried to get his beer, got back in his truck, and called his cousin.

Freddy answered on the third ring. "Wat up, cuz?"

"Where you at? I need to talk to you 'bout something dat can't wait," Cherokee said.

"I'm in tha bricks... want me to come up dere?" Freddy asked, thinking that Cherokee was at Tonya's.

"Naw, I ain't up there… Shid, dat's really why I need to holla atcha. Be on 16th in ten minutes. I'ma pick you up," he told Freddy before ending the call.

Cherokee fired up another blunt he had rolled. He rushed the blunt and downed the beer before pulling off to go pick his cousin up.

When Cherokee pulled up on 16th Avenue by the Boys and Girls Club, Freddy was nowhere in sight. Just as Cherokee reached for his phone, he saw Freddy coming out of LaSheka's house.

Freddy saw Cherokee from LaSheka's back door and ran out to the truck, trying to dodge the raindrops.

LaSheka was a "bad bitch" turned smoker. She used her project as a means to stay high. She would let different dope boys and hustlers in the hood hold dice games there, and play poker, tonk, spades, and catch their plays. She basically let them do just about anything at her crib as long as they gave her a free hit.

Freddy dipped into her spot to get out of the rain while he waited for Cherokee. He wondered what was so important that it couldn't be said over the phone. "Damn cuz, where y'all been all day?" Freddy said. "I been up there three times tryna get a sack. Tha last time, I thought I was going crazy cause I coulda sworn I heard Tonya yelling something. But I guess it was tha tv cause she neva made it to tha door. Wat's up?"

A devilish smirk crept across Cherokee's face, imagining Tonya screaming from the closet. "Look,

Freddy, it's time for us to get some real money," he said. "This nickel and dime shit we doin is barely enough to keep a nigga high. I ain't tryna be out here broke, on my ass, livin off some bitch for tha rest of my life. Wat tha song say? *Des hoes ain't loyal*... So, wat's up? You wit it, or you gon' keep pinchin off des lil eight balls to get you a half a gram of soft?"

Cherokee was a master of manipulation, especially when it came to his cousin. He always knew what to say to get Freddy to do whatever it was he was scheming.

"Yea, I'm witcha," Freddy said, not even knowing what he was agreeing to. "But where is dis shit comin from? Tonya makin some nice ends off dat shit she gettin from D-Money, and I know, as well as you do, dat ain't nan one of y'all goin nowhere."

Cherokee grabbed the ten-dollar bill resting on the armrest, unfolded it, and took a couple hits of the powder before passing it to Freddy. "Fuck her! Didn't I jus say, des hoes ain't loyal?" he said. "That goes for her too, nigga! And that nigga D-Money don't get no more passes from me. I been sparing his ass for tha longest cause he was fuckin wit Tonya on tha weed, but come find out, he been fuckin her from tha looks of it."

Cherokee ran down the details of how he found out about DeJuan and Tonya fucking around, and what he'd done to her. The only thing he didn't mention was the $3,200 he stole from her.

When he finished telling Freddy what went down, Freddy was looking at him sideways as if he didn't totally believe him.

Cherokee noticed the look and felt the energy Freddy was giving him and said, "If you think I'm bullshittin, reach up under your seat."

Freddy pulled a Kroger bag from under the seat with twelve individually bagged ounces in it.

Cherokee said, "Look back there in tha back nigga. I ain't got no reason to lie to you."

Freddy looked and noticed the truck filled with his belongings. A thought crossed Freddy's mind, and he said, "So, that wasn't the TV I heard earlier?"

Cherokee laughed, picturing Tonya again. "Fuck dat bitch! Dat's wat she get for fuckin ova a real one. Now it's D-Money's turn to feel tha wrath of a real nigga. I jus wanna make sure dat when we catch'em, we catch'em good… So, you wit me, right?" he said as he pulled off.

"Yeah, you know he be gettin it from RahRah and Smoke at tha barbershop sometimes. Shid, we can get all three of'em, if you want to, cuz. Ion give no fucks! It's all 'bout how you wanna go at it," Freddy said as he shoveled more powder up his nose.

"Dat's wat's up. We gon' put it together, but right now, we need some more soft. After we grab what we need, we can get a room and put tha play togetha. I got a couple hunid dollars. If you got seventy, eighty we should be able to grab a quarter from Rodney and be on our way," Cherokee said, heading back towards the sports bar.

Freddy reached into his pocket and pulled out a few crumpled-up twenties and a couple of fives and passed them to Cherokee as they turned onto Jefferson Street. They made it to the bar, copped what they were looking for, then headed to get a room to plot and get high.

Tonya got loose and made it out of the closet. Although she felt like crying, she simply didn't have the energy. She wondered who she could possibly tell about what Cherokee had done to her that it would actually matter to. All she could do was stare in the mirror at the beaten and bruised reflection staring back at her. She didn't have any family. At least not any that she mattered to. She wished and wanted so badly to have someone like DeJuan to step in and save her. For it to actually be him would make it that much better. But at this point, anyone would do.

The thought of DeJuan, for whatever reason, made her a little uneasy. She knew she had to tell him something because he would definitely want his money. Prolonging the conversation would only make things worse. Tonya thought he wouldn't be too upset if she just kept it real with him, considering what had happened, and the fact that since she had been getting weed from him, she had only been short with his money twice. Being that she didn't have a dime of the $1,050 for the pound that she owed him for, Tonya felt defeated, not knowing exactly how to approach and tell DeJuan her dilemma.

Chapter 10
When It Ain't Yo Night

DeJuan and TyChelle pulled up in front of Club Agenda, looking so fresh and so clean, you would've thought Big Boi and Andre 3000 had them in mind when they made their hit song. The blacker-than-black paint that DeJuan had paid $12,000 for made his Monte Carlo look as if it were melting right in front of you. The double "G" Gucci emblems seemed to jump out of the paint when the light hit the car just right, making you think your eyes were playing tricks on you. The black-and-gold 24-inch Asanti wheels set the whole look off, perfectly matching the black leather with gold stitching interior.

When DeJuan stepped out of the car, he looked like new money, straight off the press. He had on brand new black Purple Label jeans and a black V-neck with gold stripes to match his whip. The $1,100 Gucci shoes, $400 Gucci belt, and $600 Gucci shades TyChelle bought him as his gift were simple compliments to what she had on.

She stepped out in a $2,700 Gucci dress with $900 Gucci heels to match. When they entered the club together, they looked like a walking, talking Gucci ad. All eyes were on them as they moved through the crowd. Every time they stopped, either for DeJuan to dap someone up or to see who was calling TyChelle's name, the lights reflected off of DeJuan's watch and the diamonds in TyChelle's ears, almost blinding anyone looking in their direction.

As they made it to their V.I. P. booth, the DJ was right on cue. The moment DeJuan gave him the "go-ahead" nod, he cut the music saying, "The birthday boy is in the building. D-mutha-fuckin-Money, tha night is yours. Turn up, my G!"

A waitress brought over two bottles of Rose' Moet, a bucket of ice, cups, and a bottle of White Remy Martin, which was DeJuan's favorite drink. DeJuan tried to tip her but paused when he looked in the direction she was pointing and saw Smoke, RahRah, and J-Smooth at the bar raising their glasses.

DeJuan was enjoying himself and didn't think the night could get any better until he ran into Shanell. He was coming out of the restroom, heading back to his table, and unexpectedly bumped into her. He hadn't seen her in a couple of years and almost didn't recognize her.

Her shoulder-length, jet-black, curly hair was now short and dyed blonde. Being of mixed race, she had natural curly hair and never really had to do much to it before.

Looking at her, Shanell reminded him of Amber Rose. She had on a white and black Adidas T-shirt that was cut and hanging off her shoulder, some black denim shorts, and a fresh pair of shell-toe Adidas.

DeJuan had always loved her swag, and she didn't let him down. He gave her a once-over, looking at only her in the crowded club. And just like that, his mind went back to the last time he had seen her, in the back seat of her car. The thought of that night alone brought a smile to his face that he failed to keep from showing.

"Damn Dee, you gon knock me down tryna get back to wifey," she said, bringing him back to the present.

"Naw, you know I'll neva knock you down ma… you know dat. Where you been? Why I ain't seen or heard from you?" DeJuan asked.

"That's why," she said, spotting TyChelle moving quickly towards them through the crowd. She gave DeJuan a look before heading in the opposite direction.

"Wat tha hell was that about?" TyChelle said to herself as she and DeJuan headed back to their booth.

"What was what about?" DeJuan asked, reading her lips and noticing the look on her face. He already knew she had something on her mind.

"For real nigga… now you Dumbo? Naw, I know wat it is. You think cause it's yo birthday, you gon' have yo cake and eat it too! Well, not this year. But I ain't gon stand in your way, if you doin you. I most definitely ain't 'bout to stay in dis bitch wit you disrespectin me. I'm gone!" TyChelle gathered her things to leave.

"Hold tha fuck up, Chelle," he said, grabbing her by the elbow. "Ain't nobody disrespecting you. Plus, you know I don't even like cake." DeJuan was trying to lighten the mood and ease the tension.

"Fuck all dat… I ain't goin, and you know this. I'll be home when you get there. Now, let me go so I can catch a ride wit Tara."

He let go of her arm but took off behind her.

"Baby, you know if you leave, I'm leavin. You put this together for me, so wat's up?"

TyChelle didn't respond and kept moving towards the entrance of the club.

They made it outside, passing DeJuan's car parked right in front of the club, and walked through the parking lot on the side of the club. TyChelle finally stopped, not to talk, but to retrieve her phone from her Gucci bag to call to see where Tara had parked. TyChelle didn't want to be around DeJuan for the twenty minutes or so it would take them to get from the club to their house.

While she was ignoring him, he continued to try to get through to her, and neither of them noticed Cherokee and Freddy coming out of the club behind them.

Cherokee and Freddy's eyes had been on them from the time they walked through the door. This was their night to come up, and they knew they would have to be on point for them to cash in. When they saw the argument spark up inside, they felt their pockets start to fatten. Seeing

TyChelle head towards the door with DeJuan behind her, they knew it was time to put their plan into action.

Cherokee shot past them, unnoticed by the two, exiting the club to get the straps they had left in his truck. They already had stockings in their pockets that would conceal their identity, and they were both dressed in dark colors. Cherokee saw DeJuan and TyChelle stall in the parking lot, and his cousin, standing close to them, pull his stocking over his face. Cherokee did the same and approached the angry couple with his gun drawn.

TyChelle looked up and realized what was going on. Out of fear, she instinctively turned to run but was met by Freddy's fist crashing into the side of her face. She dropped to the ground.

DeJuan rushed to defend his woman, but Cherokee swung the long-barreled .357 that was in his right hand, across his head. The rubber grip made it that much easier to work with. He swung again, and after a few open gashes to the head, DeJuan was ready to comply with whatever the two goons were demanding of him.

"Wat y'all want?" he said, pulling about $6,500 from his pockets and throwing it at the gunman's feet.

"Now, dat's more like it," Cherokee said. "Lemme get dat ice, keys, and dat Gucci bag too. Do dat and y'all can enjoy tha rest of y'all night." You could see a smirk on Cherokee's face hidden underneath the stocking mask.

TyChelle and DeJuan gave the robbers what they asked for. The masked men quickly left in DeJuan's car, leaving them without a ride.

DeJuan and TyChelle went back inside to find Tara, who gave them a ride to the house where TyChelle began to nurse DeJuan's wounds.

Chapter 11
Bad Business

DeJuan stayed in the house, laid up, healing for a couple of days. During that time, he kept his ear to the streets, waiting to hear something about him being robbed the night of his birthday bash. He wanted more than anything to get some type of lead on who had violated him. He figured no one was in the parking lot when it happened, so if someone knew anything about it, then he needed it to be passed on to him. It didn't matter if they saw something, or just heard something, he wanted to know whatever it was they knew.

He was waiting for any type of information so he could take it back to the person it came from and get more answers. He was tired of the waiting game and decided to hit the streets and get back on his shit. He figured coming out and showing his face would spark people to start talking about what happened.

As he got ready to leave the house, where he had imprisoned himself, he realized that he didn't feel comfortable in the Nautica shirt, khaki pants, and Reebok classics he had on. Instead, he changed into an LRG jogging suit and a pair of Jordans before jumping into the suburban that he'd been using to go back and forth to the store and to pick Lil D up from school.

DeJuan rolled the block with the window slightly cracked to take in the fresh air that only followed a good rain. It had rained for two days straight and just stopped that morning.

Hitting north Nashville unnoticed in the suburban truck, he made his way through the Andrew Jackson Projects. He was undecided if he was going to stop by Talley's or not.

He passed Talley's street, deciding to pull up on him later. He wanted to circle the whole north side, from Andrew Jackson, 28th, Buchanan, 12th to 23rd, Dodge City, Cheatham, Jefferson Street, and back, to see what he could see before anyone realized what he was riding in.

As he rode down Jefferson Street, he slowed to peep out the sports bar and the crowd that was there. He drove past the sports bar and made a left on 28th. He got a weird feeling that something was wrong. He picked his phone up from the passenger seat and called J-Smooth.

He got no answer. When he made it to 28th and Clifton Street, he was still baffled as to why his homeboy wasn't answering. Driving down the street, he saw police putting J-Smooth into the back of one of the many squad cars that were surrounding the barbershop. He watched the young officers go in and out of the shop.

The police had people in cuffs sitting on the curb as they searched certain cars on the lot. From DeJuan's viewpoint at the red light, he saw James, Smoke, and Faye in cuffs sitting on the ground, and James and Smoke's vehicles being searched. He also saw RahRah's car on the lot, but didn't see him in the mix. As the light changed, he rolled through the intersection and then saw the police putting J-Smooth in one of the patrol cars.

He immediately called the bonds office of A-Luv bonding, a number he kept on speed dial. After several rings, the bondsman finally answered the phone. "A Luv bonding, this is Wayne speaking."

"Wayne, it's D-Money. They got my nigga in tha back of they car, prolly 'bout to take him downtown. I don't know wat they gon' charge him wit and it really don't matter, when his name pop up in tha system, I want him outta there. His name is James McCullough."

"I gotcha, Dee. Can I call you back at this number, if I need to, or to just give you an update on your guy?" Wayne asked.

"Yeah," he said before disconnecting with him. DeJuan searched his contacts for RahRah's number and called him, wondering what had happened for all this to have taken place.

"Cuz, wateva you do, don't go to tha shop!" RahRah said as soon as he answered.

"I jus passed tha shop. I see they got dat mutha-fucka shut down right now. Where you at? I seen yo whip in tha lot… you straight?"

"I'm watchin from tha store. I had jus came ova here for some cigarettes and was on my way back ova there, when they rushed dat bitch!" he said, standing on the side of the store smoking a Newport.

"Damn, for real… aight, I'm finna circle tha block and pull up on you," he said before hanging up.

DeJuan made three left turns and was pulling into the store lot before RahRah had even finished his cigarette. DeJuan hopped out of the truck. "Let me catch dat short, homie," he said, referring to the half-smoked Newport. "We can't smoke in tha rental. But fuck all dat… wat happened ove there?"

They were both focused on the barbershop.

"Man, dat shit was crazy! I had jus got out tha chair and was comin ova here to get some change cause I jus had a couple hunids. Anyway, I saw Freddy get out dat black truck right there," RahRah said as he pointed across the street at the black Dodge Ram that was on the barbershop's lot. "By tha time Freddy made it in tha shop, cars was pullin up from er'where you can imagine. White boys wit badges was jumpin out before tha cars even stopped. Cuz… it was some real movie shit!"

"Damn, so Freddy young ass dun served da vice and ran up in tha shop?" DeJuan asked, not really needing an answer. "Dat's fucked up. Damn… so wat's up, you good? I see yo car ova there."

"Iono… I'm really tryna see if they try to search it. If they do, I'm fucked. It's tre pounds on the back seat and a tre eight under tha driver seat. I guess it just depends wat they do. I know I ain't goin ova there til they gone," RahRah said, thinking about his situation.

"Well shid, roll wit me for a minute. We'll give'em time to do their job and clear out, then swang back."

They got in the rental and pulled off in the opposite direction of the commotion. They were headed back towards the projects when it dawned on DeJuan that he was going to need someone to sign off on J-Smooth's bond. While they were stopped at a red light, he texted Tara, *HMU WEN U GET FREE… I ND U 2 DO SUMN FOR ME.*

She called him back just as they were pulling in front of Talley's.

DeJuan put the truck in park and answered, "Hey Tara, wat you gon' be doin in 'bout a hour?"

"Nothing, you need me to get Lil D for a lil while?" she asked.

"Naw, I need you to get J-Smooth. He got jammed up and I need you to sign off on his bond so he can get out. You know we got you, though. Y'all straight right?" he inquired. DeJuan knew that Tara and J-Smooth had their time with one another, and if it had ended, it was on a good note.

"Yeah. We cool… he fulla shit sometimes, but we cool. Just lemme know wat I need to do," she said.

"Aight T, when tha bondsman get back at me, I'ma hit you up," DeJuan said, then hung up.

After ending the call with Tara, he got out of the truck and saw Tonya sitting on the porch. DeJuan hadn't heard from her in a few days, which wasn't like her. As he made it to the porch, he saw that she had an ugly bruise on her face.

He started not to say anything, but was met with a look that was begging him to say something. DeJuan opened Talley's door, letting RahRah go inside. He stayed with Tonya and cut through the awkward silence, saying exactly what was on his mind, "Wat happened to your face, beautiful? Don't tell me I'ma have to fuck dat nigga of yours up."

"Naw, it wasn't him," she lied. "I didn't know how to tell you, but I got robbed a couple days ago. Some niggas ran in here on me and took er'thang. I been tryna find a way to get up at least half of what I owe you, but they didn't leave a bitch nun but this." Tonya pointed to her face, which had just started to heal. She didn't want to implement Cherokee because she figured it would sound like it was something that they both planned.

"You coulda told me dat, bae. I coulda put my ear down and tried to find out something for you. Not to say it woulda did any good… hell, I still ain't heard shit 'bout tha niggas dat got me. But when I do…" DeJuan said, leaving his last statement unfinished. The thought of what he was going to do when he found out who robbed him made his palms sweat.

His phone vibrated. Looking at it, he saw that it was the bondsman. "Anyway, you know I gotcha. If yo nigga ain't gon take care of you, I guess I got to. Let me take care of this business wit J-Smooth and I'll get witcha later on, or first thing tomorrow."

Hearing those words, Tonya's energy shifted and she had a totally different look.

DeJuan answered the call on his way into Talley's. "What's up, Wayne. Talk to me."

"Yo man's bond is ready to be made. It ain't but twenty-five hundred, which you know ain't but two-fifty. Don't worry 'bout tha money. You good on that. Just have someone come down and sign him out," Wayne said.

"Aight, LaTara Hendricks will be at your office in 'bout twenty, thirty minutes. Good lookin out Wayne," DeJuan said, then disconnected the call. He called Tara and gave her the bondsman's number and filled her in on what she needed to do.

DeJuan and RahRah smoked a couple of blunts while watching Lil Mike play his homeboy Chris in a game of Madden. About an hour later, DeJuan got a call from J-Smooth asking where he was so he could have Tara drop him off.

While in the car with Tara, J-Smooth stole a few feels, rubbing on her legs and thighs, even trying to kiss her as she drove.

"Why you ain't been hittin me up, Tasty?" J-Smooth asked, using the nickname that he'd given her the first time they'd had sex. Back then, he told her that she tasted like his two favorite fruits, watermelon and pineapples combined.

"Cause you got too many hoes. All you wanna do is fuck… I ain't mad at you or nun, but I need a lil more than some dick, Smooth."

"But you do admit that you need some dick, though, right? Well, lemme know when I can put it in yo life." J-Smooth said as he got out of the car in front of Talley's. He didn't give her time to respond before closing the door.

"Wat up, nigga!" DeJuan hollered at J-Smooth, through the screen door, watching as he stepped on the porch.

"Not shit, bruh. I'm glad you had Wayne on point cause I was talkin a toilet-fulla shit when them bitches put tha cuffs on me and threw me in tha car. I told one of'em I'd be out faster than I nut when his bitch be suckin my dick… aww, he was fire hot." J-Smooth said, laughing. "So yeah, I'm glad you made it where my shit-talkin didn't turn around on me after they took me down fa dat lil ass shit. I ain't have nun but 'bout half a quarter of weed and some gars." He shook his head. "I got real raw wit they ass on tha way downtown. I told'em if they ain't got nun betta to do wit they time than waste mine, they need to find a new career, cause when I walk out that bitch before they even finish the paperwork, they gon see whose time was really wasted. But fuck all dat! Freddy weak ass caused all dat shit, runnin all up in tha shop after servin dem people."

Chris paused the game to unhook the screen and let J-Smooth in.

"I told D-Money dat nigga got straight out tha truck wit dat cracka and went straight in tha shop. Wat all he get charged wit?" RahRah asked.

"Iono, but I think he had a strap on him and some mo shit. Really, I was outta there before I found out wat I was charged wit!" J-Smooth said, getting a light from DeJuan and firing up a Newport.

DeJuan got off the couch and headed out the door with J-Smooth and RahRah behind him.

They rode back over to the barbershop to see what they missed while they were gone. RahRah's car was still parked in the lot, so he hopped out of the truck and got away from the spot, knowing that he slipped through the crack the first time. DeJuan pulled off after making sure RahRah was straight and headed to the east side to drop off J-Smooth.

Chapter 12
Try This

After meeting with Wayne to sign the papers that set J-Smooth free, Tara was back at home, sitting comfortably at her glass kitchen table. She had part of her payment divided into six lines on the table in front of her. DeJuan had given her two hundred dollars, three and a half grams of powder, and two ounces of weed.

Not bad for her just signing a couple of pieces of paper, she figured. As long as J-Smooth showed up to court, she wouldn't hear anything else about it.

With that ordeal behind her, and a little more than a gram of cocaine already in her system, Tara was feeling like a winner, with about half a gram still calling out to her from the table. Just as she was lifting the straw to her nose, about to go at one of the lines like a vacuum, she heard a knock at the door.

"Who is it?" she asked lazily as she got up to look through the peephole.

"It's me. Open tha door, girl," HP said from the other side.

Hp and Tara shared a daughter who was two years old and stayed with his mother for the majority of the time. Tara opened the door and turned right back to what she was doing before being interrupted.

HP locked the door, grabbed two glasses from the dishwasher, and sat down at the table with her. He slid Tara a glass, opened the bottle of Coconut Ciroc, and poured himself some before passing the bottle to Tara. Then he reached into his pocket and pulled out what looked like about a gram of cocaine. As he dumped some onto the table, Tara looked at what HP had, and it looked a little beige instead of the shiny white hers was. Tara was glad she had her own.

They did their thing in silence for a while until Tara finally said something, just barely breaking the silence. Her tone was much lower than usual. "Roll up a blunt," she said in a light whisper, as she hit the cigarette that she was holding. "I need to come down some. I'm high as a pair of Prada heels." She was whispering as if someone was listening, and she didn't want them to know what she was talking about.

When HP opened his eyes, he noticed hers were as big as silver dollars. He took a sip of his drink and refilled hers. In a slowed, lowered tone, HP said, "Yeah, if you jumped right now, you definitely be committing suicide." He shook his head. "Where tha cigars at?" he asked, scratching his neck and leaning back in his chair. He let his eyes slowly closed again.

"You mean to tell me, yo ass ain't got no Swisher," she asked, still quiet as a church mouse. She didn't think HP had ever been to her house and didn't have a cigar. Actually, she didn't believe there had ever been a time that she had seen him without a cigar.

"Naw, I got these white folks back on my ass for a couple years. I ain't fuckin 'round. So, naw, I ain't got nun."

"Damn," she said. Tara got up and went to her bedroom to get her rolling papers.

After rolling three fat joints, she smoked two back-to-back, downed the rest of her drink, then refilled her glass again.

Tara noticed HP rubbing his neck. "You must got some bullshit... you ova there 'bout to fall asleep. Ion think I can get any higher, you wanna hit this real shit?"

"I'm good, baby momma," he said. "And I got something that's gon' bring you down and make you feel good at tha same time." He stood up from the table and headed down the short hall to her bedroom.

HP knew his baby momma was ready to do something real freaky by the glassy look in her eyes. For Tara, sex was the icing on the cake when it came to getting high. And the nastier, the better.

HP left the kitchen. Tara assumed he went to use the bathroom, even though he said nothing to her when he left. It dawned on Tara that he was taking much longer than he normally did. She went to see what he was doing.

She found him in her bed, stretched out, stripped down to nothing but his socks. With her glass in one hand, her last joint in the other, irritated Tara said, "Get up nigga! All dat sleepy shit, you coulda did dat at yo momma house."

HP was startled by her tone. His eyelids felt like two fifty-pound sandbags, and his speech was slurred to the point he sounded like a stroke victim. "Baby Mama, I'm tryna tell you, I ain't sleep. You'll see, when you get through wit dat joint," he said with his eyes half closed.

"Ummhuh, well show me then." She put the joint out and started to peel off her clothes, revealing her petite frame, with her perky C-cups standing firm, demanding his attention.

Her nipples seemed to be begging him to reach out and touch, kiss, suck, and caress them, while her freshly shaven pussy commanded him to lick it, then stick something in it.

HP stood up, pulled her close to him. He kissed her lips, finding her tongue with his, then positioned her on the bed. She was on her hands and knees, and he began to suck on her pussy from behind. He took one pussy lip at a time into his mouth and slid two fingers in and out of her while circling her asshole with his thumb.

Tara's pussy got wetter and wetter. She threw her ass back onto HP's face and fingers. "Come on P... fuck me," she said, turning onto her back and opening her legs for him.

"Nope," he playfully told her. "You ain't runnin nothing." He grabbed the Ciroc, took a couple of sips, and dived face-first back into her wetness.

HP was stiff as a dead man but held out for a little while longer. He continued to lick her from her clit to her asshole, making her beg for the dick some more. When she started to squirm, he knew she was about to blow. He put both of her legs on his shoulders and rubbed his dick up and down her pussy lips before going in with his dick.

HP went in and out of her in that same position, making her cum three times before her legs started to shake.

He pulled out of her before he had a chance to come, but Tara was determined to fix that. She took him into her mouth, wrapping her lips tightly around him. She wasn't planning to release her grip until he released his load.

"You said you had sumn that was gon' bring me down, make me feel good… you was right," she said. "But if you doin that to them otha hoes, you betta be careful cause hoes will hurt you 'bout that type of shit." Tara got up and headed to the bathroom.

HP laughed, "You'll say any fuckin thang." He shook his head. "But dat's not what I was talkin bout."

"What was you talkin 'bout then?" she said, over the running water.

"I'll show you when you get through in there." He reached for his jeans on the floor beside the bed, and pulled out a cigarette and the powder he had been snorting earlier

After lighting a Newport, he poured the rest of the vodka into their glasses.

Tara came out of the bathroom looking at HP. "Lemme hit that cigarette baby daddy."

"Aight, but come hit dis first," he said. He put a couple small lines of the powder she had seen him with earlier on the nightstand.

"I still got some soft… I'm cool on that," she said.

"Girl, just hit it. I know you got dat glass… but it still ain't fuckin wit dis," he assured.

Tara got a straw out of the drawer, snorted one of the lines, and almost threw up before she got the straw out of her nose. "Wat's that shit?" she asked, making an ugly face.

HP passed her the Newport. "Just let me know how you feel in 'bout five or ten minutes." He leaned down and snorted the other line, hit his drink, then got up to go to the bathroom.

When he came out, less than five minutes later, Tara had nodded from what he'd given her. HP hid his heroin habit from her for close to a year, but he figured she could handle the heroin, just like the cocaine that he introduced her to. He covered her up and smoked a cigarette before going to sleep himself.

Early the next morning, HP woke up just as the first rays of sunlight came shining through Tara's bedroom window scratched at his eyelids. The first thing he noticed was that Tara wasn't in bed. He wasn't shocked and figured she would be in the kitchen cooking or in the living room doing hair. He got out of bed and headed to the bathroom to use it.

What he saw when he opened the bathroom door fucked his morning up. Tara was sitting, slumped over on the toilet, nodding, with the rest of HP's heroin pack from the small pocket of his jeans in her hand.

Their relationship was strange, but it worked for them. They didn't spend a lot of time together, and neither one of them tried to dictate what the other could or couldn't do. Their communication level was more so as good friends.

If HP was having issues with one of his female friends, it wasn't out of the ordinary for him to seek advice from Tara. When he did, she would always give her honest opinion on whatever the situation was and give him the girl's point of view without taking sides.

Although Tara didn't go to HP about her male friends, he knew they existed. She was too cute for someone not to be giving her the attention he wasn't.

What he didn't know, or believe, was that there had only been one other since him, bringing her body count to three men, counting him. HP found it hard to believe that a twenty-two-year-old who looked as good as she did and came from where she came from had only three men.

Chapter 13
Daddy's Little Girl

Tyson was having his morning cup of coffee while watching the news in the TV room designated for the guys on "South time." Lil Bruce approached the table where he was sitting and just stood there, waiting to have his presence acknowledged before saying anything. Lil Bruce knew early mornings weren't always the best time to strike up conversations with dudes, and he found that the older they were, the harder they were to read.

Tyson had known Lil Bruce since he was a "lil pup." He had kicked it with his pops, Bruce Major, and had done business with him since the drought of '99. Lil Bruce was doing sixty months for having a police issued .40 Glock on him when he got pulled over leaving the club.

As the reporter on the screen finished talking about the legalization of marijuana, Tyson said, "They been talkin 'bout this bullshit since before you and your friends started smokin tha shit… it's 'bout time. Weed ain't neva hurt nobody. But wat's up nephew? Why you up so early?"

Lil Bruce finally sat down across from Tyson and told him what was on his mind. "Unc, you know dat new nigga, Freddy?"

Tyson took a sip of his coffee, saying nothing, waiting for Lil Bruce to get on with whatever it was he was trying to tell him.

Lil Bruce could tell that Tyson didn't know Freddy, but he still went on to say, "Well, he's the tall, slim, dark skin nigga wit tha dreads and tha six golds across tha bottom of his grill. He got here Friday night."

"Yeah, I know that skinny nigga you talkin bout. Wat's up wit'em nephew?" Tyson said, putting a cigarette in the corner of his mouth while digging in his pocket for his matches.

"Him and his cousin, Cherokee, are tha niggas that robbed D-Money and your daughter, and took D-Money's car after his birthday bash last month," Lil Bruce slowly and calmly stated. He had a devilish grin on his face that seemed to grow with every word he spoke out of his mouth.

What Lil Bruce told Tyson registered so fast it felt like time froze. In his mind, he had already killed that boy six different ways before Lil Bruce had finished talking. Tyson picked up the cigarette that had fallen from his mouth and said, "Send'em my way next shift when C.O. Givens come in."

"Cool, I gotcha, Unc."

Tyson never questioned information coming from Lil Bruce. He knew he was a real one. But out of curiosity, he asked, "How you know?"

Lil Bruce grinned again and said, "Last night I rolled up a couple of joints, asked the nigga if he wanted to smoke. He from tha city, so I was gon' fuck wit'em. So once we put dat shit in tha air and rushed a pint of gas I got from tha white boys, he wouldn't shut up. He ended up tellin me er'thang 'bout tha robbery, and takin tha car, and that tha reason he's even locked up is cause he got caught wit D-Money's strap."

"This stupid mutha-fucka dun fucked up more than he know," Tyson said, nodding his head as he took in what Lil Bruce was telling him. "I gotta make a call but make sure you get him to come holla at me once Givens gets here." Tyson struck a match to light his cigarette.

Lil Bruce got up and said, "Aight, you know I got you." He turned to head to his cell.

Tyson headed back to his cell, already putting a plan together in his head. It took him half the time to get back. *This gon' be easy,* he thought. Back inside his cell, he put up his violation, a covering to block the window on his cell door so no one could see inside.

He then went to his mattress, where he kept his cellphone stuffed inside, and called TyChelle's number. "Hey, baby girl," he said when she answered.

TyChelle was glad to hear her father's voice.

"I miss you," she said. "When you think they gon' move you closer to home so I can visit you more?"

"I can't make that call, baby… but look, the reason I called is cause I need to holla at Dee. Is he around?"

"Yeah… he might still be sleep, but I'll get him up for you. Is everything alright?" She was confused as to why her father was calling to talk to her man.

"Of course it is, and it might be gettin better." Tyson thought about plugging DeJuan in with Bruce. The way he saw it, as long as DeJuan was strong in the streets, his baby girl would be safe and taken care of.

TyChelle woke DeJuan up, telling him her father wanted to speak to him.

"What's up, pops," DeJuan said into the phone.

"Not a whole lot, son. I got some shit dropped on my doorstep this morning. I'm goin to clean up on my end, but I can't reach tha flies swarming around the rest of tha shit and thought you might enjoy swattin tha mutha-fucka out tha air yourself," Tyson said.

DeJuan shook his head, lay back and said, "Wat is it? Talk to me." It was too early for him to try to decipher all of Tyson's riddles, and he wished he would just say what he'd called to say, but he would never tell Tyson that.

When he heard Tyson say, "I know who robbed you last month," DeJuan shot back up like he'd been struck by lightning.

"Yeah right," he said. "How you find out? Tha streets definitely ain't sayin nothing."

"You know a nigga by tha name of Freddy, with some golds across tha bottom?" Tyson asked.

"With dreads?" DeJuan said, knowing the answer before Tyson even said it.

"Yeah, that's tha one. Him and his cousin Cherokee did that shit. But like I said, I'ma take care of tha shit on my doorstep, which is Freddy. What you gon' do about tha otha fly?"

"I'm 'bout to go through sprayin insecticide!" DeJuan said, getting dressed in the clothes that he'd taken off only a few hours before.

"Look, when you catch that fly, call this number back and leave me a message that it's taken care of. I'ma check on something else for you. Tell my baby I love her, and Dee… make sure you catch that fly," Tyson said.

"Most definitely," DeJuan said, then the phone went silent.

Before putting the phone back into the mattress, Tyson called Bruce and told him about DeJuan. He let him know he would be giving him his number. He told him to look out for him, give him the same ticket on the work that he would give him, and to make sure that if he had any more beef, he had shooters.

Second shift came in, and Tyson sat back in his cell waiting for Freddy to come to him. He knew Lil Bruce would stay true to his word and send the youngster to him.

Not long after count had cleared, Freddy was at Tyson's cell.

Tyson let him in and introduced himself. "I'm Ty. I had my youngin' tell you to holla at me cause I heard you was alright. Plus, I like to know that er'body from tha Ville is straight. I been doin this shit for some time now, and along with making sure you got er'thang you need, I wanna make sure you know all tha rules of tha joint. The first and most important one is keep your mouth closed. When and if you open it, make sure you know who you're talkin to. That right there could save your life in a place like this. In return, not doin so could get you killed. I ain't got time to run down all tha rules to you right now, but if you follow that one rule, for the first couple of weeks you're here, until you get to know your surroundings and those around you, you'll be cool as a fan in Alaska. Right now, I gotta holla at Big Trav and Timboo 'bout some business I need them to take care of. Have you met them yet?"

"I don't think I met Timboo, but Big Trav, he tha tall ass dark skin nigga wit tha murda one right?" Freddy said as he looked around Tyson's plush cell and all the commissary that lined the walls from floor to ceiling.

"Yeah. That's him. Come down to tha weight room 'bout eight-thirty. You can meet Timboo and some more niggas on six-one-five time," Tyson said as he tossed him a little sack of weed and a pack of Newport's.

"Dat's wat's up, big homie," Freddy said. He turned and started to leave the cell.

"It ain't no thang, youngin. I'll catch up wit you later. Just remember what I said," Tyson said, walking out behind him.

Freddy headed in the direction of the yard while Tyson shot right back into his cell to retrieve what would serve as a death certificate once he put it in the right hands. He pulled out an ounce of powder cocaine, a quarter pound of weed, and a quarter ounce of heroin from his stash, then headed to Timboo and Big Trav's cell.

Timboo and Big Trav accepted the upfront payment from Tyson to take care of the business opportunity that he presented to them. What he asked for in return was for Freddy not to make it to the next count time. This task was right up their alley as they were experts in getting rid of people that certain other people felt no longer deserved to breathe.

Chapter 14
Back Riding Good

After talking to Tyson the night before and letting him know that all of his problems were behind him, DeJuan took TyChelle and Lil D out to dinner to enjoy the night with his family. Tyson had given him instructions to go by his sister's house to pick up his '96 Impala and to call Bruce first thing the next morning. He also told him that he needed to be ready to step into shoes that niggas he grew up looking up to couldn't even fill.

DeJuan felt like things were about to turn up, so he took the night to celebrate. They ate good, tripped off Lil D, and just enjoyed the evening. By the time they made it home, Lil D was knocked out in the back seat and had to be carried to his room, where he was put straight to bed.

DeJuan and TyChelle followed their son's lead, but sleep wasn't on their minds when they made it to their room.

DeJuan didn't know if it was the anticipation of the next day's events that had him wired, or not, but what he did know was that he wasn't planning on staying up alone

DeJuan knew that one of two things was about to happen. He went to grab a bottle of White Remy from the kitchen cabinet. From there, he went straight for the master bathroom where TyChelle had just stepped into the shower. He knew of the perfect way to get rid of some of that extra energy he held, and seeing TyChelle's silhouette through the shower curtain only aroused and excited him even more.

He felt like he could look at TyChelle every day for the rest of his life, and the sight of her body would always have the same effect on him. He took a few swallows of his favorite drink straight from the bottle, set it on the back of the toilet, then took off his clothes and stepped into the shower with TyChelle.

He took her washcloth from her hands and started washing her from head to toe.

Once he was satisfied, he dropped to his knees and let his mouth find the spot where her juices flowed so easily it sometimes amazed him. As he touched her, he knew that even though she was soaked from the shower, that had nothing to do with what was going on between her legs.

DeJuan lifted one of her legs over his shoulder and buried his face in her pussy, which was always clean-shaven. He sucked on her clit until it hardened, then slid two fingers inside of her. Her body tensed up and jerked a little as she started to cum.

TyChelle grabbed DeJuan by the head and pulled him up into a standing position, kissing him intensely and tasting her own juices as she did. Then she reached down, grabbed his dick, and started stroking it. She stroked it a few times before turning around to slide it between her pussy lips, filling her hole from the back just like she loved him to.

Once DeJuan was inside her warmth, there was no other place he wanted to be. He stayed there, taking long, slow strokes until he came inside of her.

Once they were done, they washed each other off again and went straight to bed. They were asleep before their heads fully hit the pillows.

The next morning, they went to TyChelle's aunt's house and got the keys to her father's car. TyChelle followed DeJuan to have the tags put in her name, then she and Lil D went their way while DeJuan headed to pick up his right-hand man, J-Smooth, and head to the car wash.

The two of them brought the candy paint back to life, making the Impala look like it had just been sprayed.

Tyson had to have paid at least $10,000 for the paint alone. It was a deep purple that looked black until the light hit it at the right angle. The twenty-inch Davins had to cost between $12,000 and $15,000 at the time he bought them.

They were on their way to Friday's to get something to eat when DeJuan remembered to call Bruce. They didn't do much talking over the phone, and there wasn't much to say. Bruce threw some numbers at DeJuan and told him he needed at least $100,000 before they could talk again.

The way those numbers sounded to DeJuan, Bruce would be seeing him real soon. DeJuan started calculating before Bruce even got off the phone. He figured that with what he already had at the house, it would only take a few quick flips for him to come up with the rest and level up and surpass the guys he grew up looking up to in the game.

The waitress placed DeJuan's steak and potato on the table, along with J-Smooth's ribs and fries, when DeJuan finally broke the silence that had come over him after speaking with Bruce.

"Bruh, we finna take tha fuck off! I just heard some shit that niggas like us only dream about. Crazy thing is, I really don't wanna change tha way we been movin," DeJuan told J-Smooth.

"Why would we switch up wat got us dis far?" J-Smooth said, sounding like he had a little sense, but not fully realizing what they would soon be dealing with.

DeJuan caught him up to speed and said, "Dude, when I get up thirty more bands, we gon be able to serve tha city… if we want."

"Wat you mean, serve tha city?" J-Smooth asked as he stopped chewing on the fries in his mouth.

"Dude I was on tha phone with, in tha car on tha way over here, is who Ty was fuckin wit before he went in, and he just gave me some unbelievable numbers. All I need to do is scrape up tha rest of tha bread," he said, signaling for the waitress to refill his Sprite.

"Well, bruh, I got like twelve bands at tha crib if dat'll get you closer to wat you need," J-Smooth told DeJuan.

"Hell yeah… Er'thang counts," DeJuan admitted. He left out that with the $12,000 J-Smooth had, he would be purchasing his own kilo of grade-A cocaine.

They finished their meal, had a few drinks, and were out. They both felt good about what they had been told. They left the restaurant and ten minutes later they pulled up to the gas station in the hood.

While DeJuan filled up the tank, J-Smooth bought the new Kevin Gates CD from the dude hustling bootlegs in front of the store. He immediately popped the disk into the CD player. As soon as the bass came in, they noticed the sound of a speaker popping.

J-Smooth turned the volume down and opened the glove box to open the trunk. DeJuan raised the trunk and saw smoke coming from the speaker box.

The car was still running. J-Smooth got out of the car and walked to the back to see what was wrong.

DeJuan instructed him to turn the car off. He could already see that the problem was coming from the sub-woofer on the far left which wasn't even screwed to the speaker box like it should have been.

The speaker was a custom-made box with three 12-inch woofers. DeJuan lifted the loose speaker and got an eye full. He quickly closed the trunk and took the nozzle out of the tank, while motioning to J-Smooth it was time to go.

DeJuan shot straight to Talley's house, and when he put the car in park, he finally turned to J-Smooth and said, "I think Christmas came a lil early this year, nigga. Watch tha street for me. I gotta get something out tha house, then we gon' celebrate if I saw wat I think I did."

DeJuan went straight in Talley's with the key he had and got the 40 Glock that he kept there, hitting Talley in his chest with an open hand as he went back out the door.

He handed J-Smooth the strap and said, "Just watch my back, bruh," as he opened the trunk and moved the woofer again. He soon realized that he wasn't seeing things. When he put his hand in the speaker box, he pulled out the square Saran-wrapped package and noticed it wasn't just one. There were two.

He took the packages straight into the house.

Talley saw what he had and his first words were, "Damn D-Money… Where we get all this dope from? Who y'all dun robbed? Want me to move dat car before tha police or somebody come through?" He was definitely confused and seeking some type of clarity.

"Naw, Unc, that's mine. Close tha door. And we ain't robbed nobody, either." DeJuan said, as he looked back, amazed at what he saw in front of him.

J-Smooth was the first to verbalize it. "Bruh, dat's two bricks, right there!" he said as he pointed at the dope.

"Yeah, that's what it looks like. Aye, Unc, grab dat weed for me." DeJuan said, realizing that he needed to sit down and think some things through. The events of the day were starting to overwhelm him.

As Talley went to get the weed, DeJuan went back outside to the car to get the cigarettes and cigars he bought before finding the hidden treasure.

While he was out there, he looked through the trunk once more and found forty thousand dollars and an AK-47 behind the speaker box.

DeJuan really didn't know what to do with everything that he found in the car. It wasn't like he didn't know who it belonged to. He needed to talk to Tyson. He searched his phone for the number Tyson had given him and left a message for him to call him asap.

Going back into Talley's, DeJuan decided to put everything up until he heard back from Tyson.

Chapter 15
Now We Ballin'

For the past month, they moved through twenty weekly kilos of cocaine and twenty-five pounds of weed that DeJuan was getting from Bruce… as sharks move through water. From the day DeJuan walked into Talley's spot with those two keys of coke, he knew things had taken a turn in his favor.

DeJuan had talked to Tyson that same evening and told him what he found, earning even more respect from him for being up front and honest. Tyson hadn't forgotten about what he put in the trunk of the Impala and gave DeJuan the green light to do what he needed to do. His only request was that he take care of his baby girl.

After talking to Tyson, DeJuan called Bruce and set up their first face-to-face meeting that Saturday.

Bruce had been out of town when they first spoke, which gave DeJuan the extra time needed to get rid of the extra coke and get up as much money as possible.

Four days later, they met at one of Bruce's spots, a condo downtown. There they stood outside on the balcony, nine stories up, overlooking the Cumberland

River. That's where Bruce made DeJuan's dreams become reality.

Bruce told DeJuan that for the $160,000 he brought, in the Nike gym bag, he would be leaving with twenty kilos of cocaine and twenty-five pounds of the best weed he'd seen in a long time.

The eleven thousand per kilo and three hundred per pound of weed was like music to DeJuan's ears. After doing the numbers like a mathematician in his head, he started telling Bruce he would bring the $67,500 as soon as he made it, but Bruce cut him off.

Bruce told him they would meet once a week at the same place and to expect the same package, as long as DeJuan came with close to $130,000. He then told him after a month or so, he could start making up the difference. That would give him time to get established and put his stamp on the streets. Bruce wasn't shy about letting DeJuan know that everything he was doing was a favor to Tyson, a fact DeJuan was already aware of.

After the ins and outs were in the air, they went back inside.

"Would you like a drink before you get going, D-Money? Paul should have everything in your trunk by now. I pay Paul and Phil well to handle things of this matter," Bruce said, referring to the doorman and valet. He walked over to the bar and poured him some VSOP Hennessy over a couple of cubes of ice.

"Yeah, I'll take a glass before I leave. No ice for me, though," DeJuan said.

They toasted to their new business relationship. DeJuan downed his drink and left.

That day changed everything for DeJuan, J-Smooth, and everyone in their circle. Instead of the one pound that Tonya was getting for $1,050, she was now getting five for $3500. Instead of DeJuan buying four-and-a-half ounces from Smoke for $3600, he was now dropping off two bricks a week to him for $36,000.

J-Smooth was still waiting on DeJuan, but he was no longer waiting on an ounce or two of powder and a few pounds of weed. He was getting five of the twenty kilos that DeJuan got every week. And neither one of them even touched weed anymore. The twenty-five pounds that Bruce supplied DeJuan went straight to Lil Mike.

Lil Mike was commander and chief when it came to the green. Between him and Talley, they also got three kilos of cocaine.

That left DeJuan with ten kilos to play with for the week, and he wasn't playing at all. He was getting it gone… making them fly like birds trying to get from Chicago to Panama in October. Whatever he had left before meeting with Bruce again, he locked it in a safe at a storage facility. A unit he paid his cousin to get for him under a fake name, with a fake ID that he'd gotten through Bruce.

DeJuan was pulling off Crest Cadillac's lot in a brand-new SRX that he had bought for TyChelle, with J-Smooth following close behind in the Escalade he had bought for himself.

Business was good. Even though they had seen more money in the past month than a lot of people see in a lifetime, they didn't want to go overboard with their spending, but of course, they still treated themselves.

DeJuan did so by starting Lil D a trust fund with $75,000, which would collect interest for the next thirteen years. He bought TyChelle a $30,000 engagement ring and a $45,000 SUV that he was about to surprise her with. He also stashed a $100,000 nest egg at the house. The $100,000 was his personal security blanket, and he didn't want to be too far away from it at any given time.

J-Smooth moved his mother into a nice two-bedroom, one and a half bath house with a two-car garage in a nice neighborhood. The sales price was $130,000.

RahRah entered the barbershop before the first set of clippers had even been turned on. "Wat up, Smoke? Wat's cracken, homie?"

"Not much, cuz, you good? It's early as fuck. What you got going?" Smoke replied, seeing that RahRah had something on his mind. That wasn't too hard to read.

RahRah wasn't the early morning type and usually only came to the shop when business called him to do so.

"I wanted to holla atcha 'bout D-Money. I know he was gettin his work from you, not dat I was tryna be in y'all wax and shit, but since dat shit happened on his birthday, it seems like… Iono… shit's changed wit'em. Plus, he was snatchin P's from me on schedule damn near three times a week… he ain't hollered my way in a month or so," RahRah said.

Smoke knew exactly what RahRah was talking about and was just as confused about what DeJuan was doing. It was plain to see to anyone with eyes that he was still taking care of business. "All I can say is, by robbin that nigga, they only pissed him the fuck off, cause he been goin hard as a brick ever since. He threw me for a loop when I asked him when he was gon' need to holla at me, cause like I said, since he came out after his birthday, ya boy been good… real good. He asked me what I was payin and turned 'round and gave me a ticket I couldn't refuse. It's a few niggas out here he fuckin wit, but as far as I can tell, er'body else gon' starve, cause even though he movin some weight, he still piecing shit together like a jigsaw puzzle too," Smoke said as he set up his station and turned the flat screens and lights on in the shop.

Putting everything together, RahRah said, "So, D-Money tha man now… Maybe he can get tha green a lil cheaper too then. Dat's wat's up, cuz. I'll get witcha later. I'm out."

He left with a whole new picture of D-Money painted for him.

Chapter 16
Old Flames Never Die Out

Kandace had gone to Lime Lite around 8 p.m., planning to have a few drinks before happy hour ended and be back home and in her bed by 10. It was well past that when she noticed the time and recognized a face that she hadn't seen in years.

She was chilling at her table when her longtime friend Tiffany saw her. They had been like sisters for about ten years, inseparable from first through tenth grade. That's when Kandace got pregnant and couldn't keep up any longer. However, they continued to be super cool. But Kayla, Kandace's daughter, became her main focus, whereas Tiffany was focused on having fun, being fly, and fucking DeJuan as much as possible. That was, until she graduated and left for college in Virginia.

DeJuan had taken Tiffany's virginity during her freshman year of high school, when he was a sophomore. It was one of the many days he didn't feel like being at Pearl Cohn. He and Kandace were both staying with his grandmother at the time, right across the street from the school. When Tiffany came looking for Kandace around lunchtime, he gave her a sample of what sex was like.

For the next two years, they would creep off and "do them," as much as they could. Tiffany knew DeJuan had a girlfriend and several other girls he messed around with besides her.

Because Tiffany wasn't big on drama, she never said anything to anyone, not even to Kandace. She didn't want anyone thinking she was stupid or judging her, especially knowing how DeJuan got down. That's exactly what Kandace said later, after DeJuan finally told her he was fucking her best friend.

Now that they were grown, Kandace realized she didn't have a dog in the fight. They exchanged hugs, caught each other up on life, then Tiffany popped the question that Kandace already knew in the back of her mind would be asked. "So, what's DeJuan been up to?"

"Tha same shit. Still in tha streets," Kandace said coldly, finishing her drink.

To Tiffany, that was good news. It meant he might still be out. "You think you can call him for me and tell'em that an old friend wants to see him if he ain't too busy."

"Yea, I can call him, but I don't know…" Kandace started, not bothering to finish what she was about to say. She knew exactly why Tiffany wanted to see him.

As Kandace scrolled through her contacts finding his number. She noticed her battery was about to die.

Instead of calling, she used Tiffany's phone to send a text, since it was so loud in the club.

After sending the text, she asked Tiffany where she was staying and how long she'd be in town. Seeing that Tiffany was only in town for the weekend and Kayla was at her grandmother's, they decided Tiffany would stay with her.

When DeJuan got the text, *CUZ… I GOT SUMBDY TRYNA C U…* he instantly called. Kandace told Tiffany to watch the table while she took the phone and headed to the bathroom, where she could hear.

"Damn, that was fast," she said into the phone as she answered.

"Yeah, cause I ain't got time to waste. Who numba is dis and who you talkin 'bout tryna see me?" DeJuan asked, getting straight to the point.

"My bad mister big shit poppin… I thought I was talkin to my cousin," Kandace said.

"Cuz, quit playin… wat's up?"

"Tiffany is here and wanna see you."

"Tiffany?"

"My best friend Tiffany, yo old cree-cree."

"Yea right! Where y'all at?" DeJuan asked when it finally registered.

"Keep it in your pants nigga! We 'bout to leave Lime Lite and head to my house. Meet us there in 'bout thirty minutes," Kandace said.

"You gotta come get me, cuz." DeJuan never drove his cars to his cousin's house if he planned on being there longer than ten to fifteen minutes. He knew he would be a sitting duck, in the wrong pond, if he did, because so many people knew her.

"I knew you was gon' say dat shit. Well, you gotta pay me."

"Yeah, and I knew you was gon' say that. I gotcha though. I'm in A.J., on Blank. Call me when you get close."

They hung up.

Kandace made it back to the table just as the round of drinks Tiffany ordered arrived. She told her she would go get DeJuan and meet her at the house, gave her the keys to get in, and her phone, then headed out of the club.

As she pushed the button to start her shadow black Altima, Beyoncé came blasting through the speakers and had her feeling herself.

Before making a right onto Blank Street, she called DeJuan, "Come on out nigga."

When she pulled up in front of Talley's, DeJuan was already on the porch waiting. It was sprinkling, but that didn't make the hot day any cooler. DeJuan made it to the car, got in and threw his LRG jacket he was using to block the rain into the back seat. Since he already knew his cousin's rules about smoking weed in her car, he searched his pockets until he found his cigarettes, then fired up a Newport.

"Gimme my twenty and a cigarette," Kandace said as she jumped on the interstate.

She was the only person who made DeJuan feel like wearing his seatbelt wasn't optional, but mandatory.

Kandace put 8-Ball and MJG's Space Age Pimpin on, called Tiffany to let her know they were on their way and smoked a cigarette.

DeJuan took a peek at the speedometer and noticed they were doing 94 mph. He knew she would only snap at him if he tried to tell her anything about her driving. He just let his seat back and looked out the window. That's when he saw the blue lights behind them.

Kandace noticed them at the same time. "Wat tha fuck they want?" she said, like she wasn't doing thirty miles over the speed limit.

DeJuan would have been in disbelief had someone else said that, in the same predicament, but he knew his cousin. He shook his head as she pulled to the side of the road and got the title, proof of insurance, and her license ready for the police officer that was walking up to her window. DeJuan knew she was legit, so he didn't have a worry in the world… until he heard the words that shot out of her mouth towards the police officer.

"Wat tha fuck you pull me ova fa? I'm tryna go home, where yo pink ass need to be… y'all kill me wit dis bullshit!" Kandace shouted before the officer could say anything.

Hearing her, the officer instantly said, "Cut the car off and step out of the car ma'am."

He had already called for backup, figuring Kandace was under the influence.

DeJuan was reaching for his wallet to show the officer his license when he felt the gun on his hip that had somehow slipped his mind. At the same time, he noticed another officer standing at his door.

"Step out of the car," the officer said.

DeJuan could tell by the tone of his voice and his demeanor what was next. DeJuan went with his first instinct and bolted as soon as his Chuck Taylors hit the ground. He immediately regretted that he didn't put on a different pair of shoes that morning.

His mind didn't stall there for long, as it was preoccupied with getting away, or at least getting rid of the .45 that he was clutching. He darted through some bushes, jumped a fence, and ended up behind an apartment complex. Once he saw that the middle-aged policeman was no match for his speed and agility, he didn't throw the gun, but did stash it underneath a broken-down Chevy S-10 that looked like it hadn't been moved in over a year or so, and wasn't going to be moving anytime soon.

He kept moving. It wasn't until he felt the light raindrops that started to fall that he thought about his jacket that he'd left in Kandace's back seat. He stepped into the breezeway of one of the apartment buildings and sat on the step. "Shit!" DeJuan knew the police were going to take his cousin to jail and end up charging her for the twenty-three grams of weed that was in the pocket of his jacket.

DeJuan fired up a cigarette and dialed the number that Kandace had texted him from.

"Hello," Tiffany answered.

"I need you to come get me," DeJuan said.

"D-Money?" she said, confused.

"Yeah."

"I thought Kandace was pickin you up. I'm at her house waitin on y'all," she said, confused on what was happening.

"I know, I know. Now it looks like we gotta go get her," DeJuan said through a cloud of smoke as he exhaled.

"I don't understand, but where are you?" Tiffany grabbed her keys and Kandace's house key. She was in the car when it dawned on her what apartments DeJuan was talking about. "Okay, gimme 'bout ten minutes. I'm on tha way," she said.

Eight minutes later, DeJuan saw headlights turn into the complex just as his phone vibrated. "Is that you, in that red Q45?" he asked as he put the phone to his ear.

"Yeah, boy. Where you at?" Tiffany said, looking around for him.

DeJuan spooked her as he ran up on the passenger side while her head was turned looking in the opposite direction.

He jumped in the car. "Damn girlfriend… tha shit I gotta go through to see yo ass. Where you been?"

"Fuck you boy. Where is Kandace?" she said.

"Prolly downtown, by now. She got pulled ova on our way to her spot. I had to bounce cause I had a lil toaster on me… matter of fact, I need to grab it before we head to get her. Pull down by that lil white truck, right there," he said, pointing to the S-10.

She pulled into the parking space beside the truck, and DeJuan got his gun and got back into her car. He then called the bondsman to have them check on Kandace's charges. DeJuan told Tiffany to hold up before pulling off while he got the details of Kandace's charges.

This was the exact reason Tiffany loved fucking with DeJuan. It was the excitement that came along with him, not knowing what his next move would be at any given moment. But at the same time, knowing for sure that it wasn't going to be a dull one.

As he talked to the bondsman, she went after what she wanted. She felt for his manhood growing through his jeans. She bypassed his zipper and had a limp six inches in her hand, stroking it to a hardness that she had been missing for longer than she knew. By the time DeJuan was done with his call and laid the phone down, he was ready to start on Tiffany.

He reached over her lap, moved the lever up on the side of her seat, letting it back and making it recline. Tiffany knew it was about to go down and helped him ease her skirt up, freeing her of the red thongs she had on. He tried to climb over and get in where he could fit, but she moved quicker than he did. She mounted him in his seat, allowing him to fill her hole, and satisfy her desires at the same time. She grinded her hips all the way to an orgasm in less than five minutes. It didn't help that she had built up anticipation stored away for DeJuan.

Once she had cum, she climbed back into the driver seat and said, "So what now?"

"Now we go to cuz house and finish wat you started, cause they gon' hold her for twelve hours for being over tha limit," he said.

They fixed themselves and did just that.

They were at Kandace's house, going at it like teenagers for close to an hour when the ringing of DeJuan's phone broke through the sounds of their sexcapade. He allowed it to go to voicemail, seeing that it was the bondsman and he'd already spoken to him, he figured there couldn't be any new information he could possibly tell him.

DeJuan was ass naked, sweating bullets, tired, and breathing hard, with Tiffany in the same condition, still on top of him when he finally reached for his phone. When he called the bondsman back, he heard, "DeJuan?" immediately coming from the other end of the phone.

"Yeah, it's me. Wat's up, Wayne?" DeJuan asked as he slid from underneath Tiffany. He sat on the side of the bed and fired up a Newport.

"I wanted to let you know that you have a warrant out for your arrest," Wayne said.

"Wat? How?" DeJuan didn't understand.

"Listen… it just went into the system. Evidently, it had something to do with your cousin's situation. The charges are fleeing and possession of…" Wayne was saying before DeJuan cut him off again.

"Possession of wat?"

"Chill," Wayne said. "Let me finish. After you took off, they searched the car and found a quarter ounce of powder and twenty-three grams of weed in a jacket on the back seat and your wallet in the passenger's seat. They easily matched you with your license and put the warrant out immediately."

"Fuck!" DeJuan wanted to smack himself when he remembered leaving his jacket in the car. He shook his head, thinking about the quarter ounce he was waiting for someone to come get when Kandace pulled up. "So wat can I do 'bout this tonight, if anything?"

"Meet me downtown in an hour, and you can be out half an hour later," Wayne said.

"Cool." They hung up.

2:43 a.m. was the time when DeJuan looked at the clock on the night table in Kandace's guest room. He and Tiffany just added another night to remember to the long list of memories they already shared.

"Shit," DeJuan said, getting up and going into the bathroom, taking his phone with him. "Girlfriend, see if you can find some clean sheets. We gotta go," he said to Tiffany before closing the door to the bathroom and calling TyChelle.

TyChelle answered after four rings, and he could tell by the tone of her voice she had been in a deep sleep. TyChelle noticed the time and said, "Why you ain't here?"

"I had to run from tha police, and now I gotta go turn myself in and make bond. Tha shit sounds fucked up, and is, but I'll explain all that. Right now, I just need you to meet me downtown to sign my bond," he told her.

"Okay, bae, I'm gettin up now." TyChelle was out of bed, and the house, and was heading downtown within five minutes of hanging up the phone. She had Tara, who was still up, keep an eye on Lil D while she was gone.

Wayne worked his magic and had TyChelle and DeJuan back at the house in less than an hour's time.

Chapter 17
Small World

DeJuan had just hopped in his new CTS Cadillac, about to leave the barbershop, when his phone started vibrating on his hip. He answered without looking to see who it was and heard an excited J-Smooth in his ear.

"Bruh, you ain't gon' believe who I'm staring at right now!"

"Who nigga?" DeJuan asked, pulling into traffic on 28th.

"Dat nigga, Cherokee," J-Smooth said.

"Yeah right, fam. Where you at?" DeJuan replied, rubbing the scar above his left eye. Just thinking about how badly he wanted to get his hands on the person responsible for the seven stitches he needed to close the wound, that left a lifetime scar for him to remember the incident by, made his blood boil.

Since DeJuan could never forget the particulars of that day, he knew he wouldn't sleep comfortably until he saw to it that Cherokee was dealt with.

"I'm down here at tha sports bar. Tha nigga jus walked in like he ain't got a care in tha world. I think he lookin for some flake. He was hollin' at Rodney 'bout sumn… Rodney nodding in my direction. I'ma hit you back, he comin ova here," J-Smooth said.

"Aight, don't let dat nigga out yo sight!" DeJuan shouted before the call was disconnected. He floored it, swerving through traffic trying to get to Jefferson Street.

He pulled into the alley behind the sports bar in what seemed like a few heartbeats. From where he parked, he spotted Cherokee's Tahoe parked in the lot across the street from the sports bar. DeJuan knew that the day had finally come when he would be able to repay him for the birthday gift he'd given him across his face. He could hardly contain himself.

Enough time passed for the physical wounds to heal, but the only way DeJuan felt he could repair the emotional damage was to make an example to show he was not to be fucked with, and eliminate the one who crossed that line from the jump.

Before he made a move, knowing that J-Smooth was keeping Cherokee occupied, DeJuan made a phone call.

"Aye, Lil Mike, I gotta check fa ya if you can take care of a lil light work fa me," DeJuan said when Lil Mike answered.

"Anything, fam… you know I gotcha. Wat you need me to do?" Lil Mike said, taking his food from the girl at Popeyes drive-thru.

"How far are you from tha sports bar?" DeJuan wanted to know before telling him exactly what he needed him to do.

"I'm right up tha street… wat's up?"

"Cool… pull down here, but park at tha Dollar Store lot. I want you to follow that nigga Cherokee when he leave tha spot and let me know where he goes." DeJuan said, grabbing and lighting a Newport to smoke while he waited for Lil Mike to pull up.

Lil Mike put the top up on his black Camaro SS that he just bought the day before, got sideways as he hit Jefferson Street, with his three-piece on the passenger seat. He got to the light at 18th Avenue and Jefferson Street and called DeJuan back. "D-Money, I'm at tha light by Paul's now, but I ain't got no heat wit me. Do I need to fix dat?" he asked.

"Naw, you good, lil bruh. I just need to find out where this bitch stayin for now," DeJuan said with a grin, seeing that Lil Mike was solid and willing to put in work if needed. But this was something DeJuan was going to take joy in doing himself, and he didn't want to be deprived of any of it.

DeJuan reached under the seat and grabbed the snub-nose .357 that he had specifically for times like this.

Once it was in the palm of his hand, he couldn't wait to put it to use. He looked up and saw Lil Mike back into a parking space across the street and knew the wait was over.

His phone rung just as he was thumping his cigarette out the window. Answering, he said, "Jus stay right there… dat bitch gon' be runnin, and jumpin in his truck in just a minute. Don't lose'em, fam."

"I gotcha, bruh." Lil Mike tossed a bone out the window.

DeJuan called J-Smooth. As soon as he answered, J-Smooth said, "Bruh, I was jus finna hit you. Dat nigga gotta half from me and went in tha bathroom."

"Good… I'm on tha way through tha back. Jus follow my lead. You know I gotta make a statement."

Once inside, DeJuan met J-Smooth's eyes. Cherokee was in the men's room for about five more minutes before DeJuan heard him running water. When the water stopped, Cherokee came out the door and was met with the butt of the .357.

An eye for an eye, DeJuan thought. He grabbed Cherokee by the collar and pulled him back to a full standing position. The first blow he threw didn't draw blood, but it did make Cherokee's knees buckle, bringing him back to earth. Coming out of the bathroom, he was high as a spaceship trying to get to the moon.

DeJuan walked to the middle of the bar, dragging Cherokee as he went, with the barrel to his head.

J-Smooth fell in line and followed suit, patting Cherokee down, taking a .380 from his back pocket.

DeJuan dropped Cherokee to the floor with a blow to the head that sent blood flying halfway across the bar. He started talking to him. "Nigga, you thought you was jus gon' fuck up my birthday and walk tha same streets as me? You got me fucked up!" DeJuan said, as he continued to rain down on Cherokee's head with blows from the .357. He opened him up, with deep gashes, in different places each time.

When he finally stopped, he doubted Cherokee's mother would even recognize him. DeJuan cocked the hammer back on the pistol and put it to Cherokee's head and said, "Look bitch… this yo lucky day. But I'ma tell ya right now, gambling is a bad habit, and I'll put yo life on it that you don't wanna see me tomorrow, tha next day, or any otha day, once you leave up outta here!" DeJuan went into Cherokee's pocket and took everything. He threw his keys out the door and gave him another gash on the back of his head as he stumbled out.

DeJuan gave the five hundred and forty dollars, and the rest of the half ounce of powder he took from Cherokee's pockets to Rodney for the disturbance.

J-Smooth stared at DeJuan with a confused look on his face. DeJuan knew exactly what was on his mind. They were out back before either one of them said anything. DeJuan spoke up first. "Don't even say it. You know I ain't through wit dat nigga. Lil Mike is following him now. You jus meet me at my house in 'bout an hour."

"Bet, I knew he wasn't gettin off dat easy afta puttin hands on Chelle," J-Smooth said as he hit the unlock button on his keypad and hopped into the Escalade.

DeJuan took off the Akoo shirt that he was wearing since it had blood on it. He used it to wipe the blood from his hands and the gun before giving the .357 to J-Smooth.

J-Smooth hit a couple of buttons on the radio, then dropped the gun into a secret compartment, closed it, and pulled off in the same direction that DeJuan had gone. It wasn't thirty minutes later when Lil Mike called DeJuan with Cherokee's location. Cherokee was on the south side of town.

Later that evening, after the sun had gone down, DeJuan pulled up at the motel a couple of doors down from the room Lil Mike said Cherokee was in. Wasting no time, DeJuan and J-Smooth got out of the car dressed in dark clothes. They went at the task at hand, like professional cat burglars. But the only thing they planned on taking was the life of a nigga they felt no longer deserved to breathe the same air as them.

J-Smooth kicked the door in.

DeJuan went inside the room with his gun drawn, ready to squeeze, and caught Cherokee at the table in his boxers, trying to snort a line of coke with a rolled-up dollar and a bloody nose.

They snatched him up quickly and left. They had him tied up in the trunk of DeJuan's car. Lil Mike followed closely behind them. They made it to a warehouse by the river where the torture of Cherokee began. It all ended with Cherokee in the Cumberland River.

Chapter 18
Vacation

It was the latter part of November, and another day of court for DeJuan. Getting out of bed that morning, he wasn't at all worried about what was going to happen in court. His lawyer had already assured him he'd be getting probation. But there was just something about the day that felt… off.

Sitting at the kitchen table, eating his breakfast, his mind shifted back to prior court dates and what the D.A. had been saying about the case. DeJuan was charged with possession with intent to distribute, tampering with evidence, and evading arrest. During his last two court appearances, the district attorney had been adamant about seeing to it that DeJuan served some real time. His lawyer, Percy, was still saying he was going to get him through the case without serving a day in jail, since it was his first felony.

DeJuan finished his sausage, cheese omelet and waffles, then headed to the bedroom and pulled out an ash grey Michael Kors suit from the closet. He paired the suit with a black and grey tie and a black Armani shirt with grey buttons and stitching. He grabbed the black Armani shoes that were stacked in the closet, amongst the many pairs of designer shoes he had, to top off his ensemble.

"Baby, can you grab my towel?" TyChelle shouted from the bathroom as she rinsed off in the shower. "I hope this tha last time we gotta go to court," she added, hearing him enter the bathroom.

"Me too, babe," he said, placing the towel on the toilet and grabbing his toothbrush.

They finished in the bathroom, got dressed, then worked together to get Lil D out of bed and into some clothes.

They took Lil D to Kandace's house, dropped him off, and headed downtown.

Sitting in the second row of the courtroom, waiting for his name to be called, both DeJuan and TyChelle sat quietly, lost in their own thoughts. The docket was still being called when Percy Clemens entered the courtroom and motioned for DeJuan to step out. They both rose and indiscreetly followed him into the hallway to hear what he had to say.

"How are you this morning, DeJuan?" Percy asked, extending his hand.

DeJuan gripped his lawyer's hand, giving it a firm shake and said, "Depends on what you have to tell me. So… how am I doing, Percy?" He used his lawyer's first name, something Percy had insisted on DeJuan doing since DeJuan had given him the $8,500 retainer to take the case.

"Well, let me just say there's a storm threatening, and there's a possibility of flooding, and the only way I can help you is by suggesting that you cut your losses and cut them early." Percy said, confusing DeJuan and TyChelle.

DeJuan was trying to make it make sense when TyChelle spoke up.

"I'm sorry but we don't know wat that's supposed to mean. Is this our last court date or not, and if not, when should we expect to be coming back?"

"Okay, keeping it simple, there's a new D.A. working the case, and she's working it like she has something to prove. DeJuan, your possession charge carries three to fifteen, and the misdemeanor evading carries eleven-twenty-nine, at most. Now, where the last D.A. was offering you six months for the fleeing, and three years' probation for the possession, she's not. She wants to see to it that you serve time on both charges. And for the possession… she won't be aiming for the minimum three years." Percy spoke clearly, ensuring DeJuan understood what he was telling him.

"Damn… so how much time am I looking at?" DeJuan asked.

"If we deal with her, you'll be looking at doing five to eight, but right now, I can still get you the deal that was on the table at your last court appearance. That's the six months, day for day, and three years' probation. Let me know when I come out of here what you want to do." Percy said. He flipped through the paper's in his hands, then headed back into the courtroom.

"I still don't understand, baby. I know he ain't sayin what it sounds like he sayin, cause he told us he was going to get you probation, and you wasn't gon' have to do no time cause it was your first case," TyChelle said. She was mad as hell, almost to the point of tears.

"I know, Chelle, but you heard him, jus like I did. There's a new D. A.…." DeJuan said, right before TyChelle cut him off.

"So fuckin wat! Tha law still tha same," She angrily said.

"Yeah, it is. And I still broke tha mutha-fucka! Not only did I break it, I got caught and admitted to it. So even though that "no time" shit sounded good, I knew and still know that every day when I'm doin wat I'm doin, there's possible time that comes with tha shit. So, I'm finna go in here and let Percy know tha business. Six months ain't shit compared to what this otha asshole talkin bout. I'ma gon' get dis shit behind me, get out and be ready to make one of two choices; either get back to it, or get out tha way. But wat I ain't finna do is whine and cry like no bitch 'bout some shit that I did. Now, what is you gon' do?" DeJuan said, pissed, thinking about the choices he had.

"You know I'm with you one hundred percent of the way, baby. But I'd be lying to myself, and you if I didn't say that I don't want you to go away… not even for a day. What am I goin to do while you're…" TyChelle couldn't even finish her statement. Tears started to roll down her face and her words got caught in her throat.

"Baby, do tha same thing you do every day. Take care of my son, chill, and be beautiful. Your job ain't changed. There's money in tha safe if you need it, and we're so far ahead on tha bills that when I get out and we go to buy our house, NES gon' owe us some bread. So, get that wet shit off your face. You ain't got nothing to worry bout. Plus, J-Smooth gon' look out for you and you know Kandace and Tara are team players that are only a phone call away.

"I guess," she said, wiping the tears away with the back of her hand. She gave her man one last hug and kiss, preparing herself for what was next.

They finally let each other go, then went back into the courtroom where DeJuan signed for his time, got cuffed, and was escorted to a holding cell.

Chapter 19
Home Alone

For the week or so since DeJuan accepted his time, TyChelle had just been moping around the house. She simply wasn't feeling like herself and was trying to find the strength and energy to get back into the swing of things.

Standing in the shower, letting the water run over her body, she wondered if she had it in her to be what DeJuan needed her to be. The fact that she still hadn't found the courage to answer Lil D honestly when he asked where his daddy was, without tearing up, told her she was fighting an uphill battle.

Lil D had been at Kandace's house since the court date. TyChelle needed time and space to take care of some business and tie up some loose ends for DeJuan. As she got ready to pick up Lil D, she wondered how she was going to finally tell him where his father was.

TyChelle stood in her walk-in closet, trying to decide between a pair of Reebok classics and some white and pink Air Force 1's, when her phone rang. "Wat's up bitch?" she heard Crissy say as she answered.

"Not shit, hoe. I was 'bout to step out for a minute. I gotta pick up Lil D and do a lil runnin around," TyChelle said.

"That's cool. So when you comin through here to get this wat I got for y'all?" Crissy asked, wondering if TyChelle had forgotten about the $3,500 that she had been telling her she was coming to get for close to a week.

Lil Mike was handling his end with the weed, giving Crissy five pounds on the strength of DeJuan. All TyChelle had to do was pick up the cash. Even though DeJuan left TyChelle stacked up with more than $150,000 in their home safe, Lil Mike still felt obligated to let him know that his loyalty didn't die when the judge gave him those six months. He wanted to make sure it was understood that if he needed him, he would still be there, no matter what.

"Gurl," TyChelle paused, trying to make sure she got the combination right on the safe, "I'm coming by there first. Why don't you ride wit me, if you ain't busy." She put the $2,500 back in the safe that she'd taken out to give Kandace. She wanted to show her appreciation for her helping out with Lil D and simply being her.

"I can do that. Jus call when you on tha way," Crissy said before they ended the call.

TyChelle turned to grab the cash from her purse on the bed. The doorbell rang. She headed out of the bedroom, down the hall, towards the front door. It rang again just before she got close enough to look out the peephole. She wasn't expecting anyone and instinctively said, "Who is it?" She was thinking it would be Tara or maybe even J-Smooth.

Before that thought exited her mind, the door crashed in on her, knocking her to the floor. Two masked men with guns rushed inside her home. The smaller one secured the door the best he could, while the larger one snatched TyChelle up from the floor.

TyChelle looked like a ragdoll in the hands of the large man as he drug her towards the bedroom, following the smaller masked man. The smaller man was the only one who spoke.

"Look hoe! We can do this tha hard way, or tha easy way, but best believe it's gettin done! Now, I know yo nigga left you straight. Give us tha cash and you can live to see tomorrow. Try to hold back one dime, and you'll regret it, and pay for it with your life!" he warned.

"But…"

SMACK.

POW.

The larger goon spun around and hit TyChelle across the head with the pistol in his right hand. The impact caused the Glock to go off, accidentally shooting TyChelle. The sound of the gunshot along with the sight of TyChelle added a sense of urgency to the situation for the two masked men.

TyChelle's body went limp in the big goon's hands. As soon as he let her go, she fell to the floor with blood covering her face and head.

"Shit! I didn't mean to shoot her, but we still finna get this bread. Let's hurry up and find it and get tha fuck outta here!" he said to his partner. He picked up TyChelle's purse from the bed and emptied out the contents, pocketing the stacks of fifties.

The smaller masked man started going through the drawers, then went straight for the walk-in closet.

"Bingo! Grab a couple of those pillowcases. Here's wat we came for," he said, as he looked into the open safe that was filled to capacity with nothing but hundreds and fifties. They cleaned out the safe and left the home through the back door, with the pillowcases in hand.

Count cleared, and DeJuan and his cellie made their way out of their cell into the pod. His cellie, Tony, a.k.a. Tiger, went straight to the T.V. room to catch the game. DeJuan headed for the phones.

After about twenty minutes, it finally got around to being his turn to use the phone. He dialed TyChelle's number four times, and each time it went to voicemail on the first ring. It had been three days since he talked to her, and he was starting to get worried.

Emanuel "MainSwang" Sharp walked straight up to DeJuan and strongly said, "Lemme get dat phone."

DeJuan just ignored him, not knowing who he was talking to. He hung up and tried to call back, and again TyChelle's phone went to voicemail.

"Damn nigga, you must can't hear. I said lemme get dat horn!" MainSwang said, raising his voice.

Looking over his shoulder, DeJuan realized that this guy, that he didn't even know, was talking to him. MainSwang's cellie, Lucci, was making laps around the pod and was within earshot.

"You can take some of dat bass out yo voice. I'll be off in a minute, even though I ain't been on tha mutha-fucka yet."

Lucci heard DeJuan raising his voice to the level that MainSwang was speaking. He came to a stop, when he realized DeJuan was talking loud to his cellie knowing MainSwang was a loose cannon.

"Wat tha fuck you mean, take tha…" MainSwang was saying, stepping closer to DeJuan when Lucci stepped between the two and cut him off.

"Wat's goin on, cuz?" Lucci asked.

"Dis nigga got tha game fucked up! Dat's all. He mus think he runnin sumn. But I'm 'bout to show'em who runnin shit!"

DeJuan let the phone drop, turned around and said, "You ain't showed me dat you run shit but yo mouth so far nigga. Wat's up!"

"D-Money? Wat up nigga?" Lucci said, recognizing DeJuan before turning to MainSwang and saying, "Hold up homie."

"Rell? Well damn," DeJuan said, realizing who Lucci was.

Lucci's real name was Terrell Stevens. He and DeJuan went to high school together, but they hadn't seen each other since. Lucci's sister, Shanell, who DeJuan had a thing with, had also gone to school with them. Lucci motioned for DeJuan to walk with him. As they started walking, DeJuan asked, "You know dat nigga?"

"Not really… met'em in here. But cuz aight. He jus always seem like he got some typa point ta prove," Lucci said.

"Shid, he was 'bout to have to prove he can fight, cause I ain't tryna talk to nobody but my gal. Yeah, I was 'bout to see if you hadn't walked up."

"I guess you ain't changed much… still TTG," Lucci said, laughing as they continued making laps.

"Naw, I ain't wit tha shit Rell. But you know I ain't goin fa nun of dat he got goin. You know how I move…

I'm gon be trained to go til the day I go… but wat's up wit you? I thought you was in Knoxville hoopin for UT," DeJuan said, as he remembered hearing that Lucci had gotten a full scholarship to play basketball.

"Yeah, you know… shit happens. I fucked my knee up tha summer before last, so they took tha scholarship back. I been grindin ever since, gettin it how I live. Dat's how I ended up in dis mutha-fucka. I was in tha trap 'bout to cook up, when my lil homie came in talkin 'bout tha vice was out. I looked out tha window and saw them hoes comin straight for tha spot. I had just enough time to make it from tha kitchen window to tha bathroom to flush tha three zips before they kicked tha door in and put er'body on tha floor. All they had left to charge me with was 'bout a gram of hard that was on tha kitchen table, two blunts I had rolled, and 'bout half a zip of weed. Ohh, they got a strap from under the couch too. Even though my nigga, Tiger, tha only mutha-fucka who had something on him, and tha house ain't in none of our names, they charged er'body wit tha lil shit dey found in dat bitch. Me, Tiger, and my homegurl Pretty C."

Lucci ran down his situation.

"Damn! Yeah, dat's fucked up. But you oughta come out aight when it's all said and done."

"Aw yeah… I'm straight. If Skeeter, tha nigga whose name is on tha house, act like he don't wanna take tha charges, Pretty C already said she'll take tha gun. Dat lil gram and weed ain't shit… I'm jus waitin on my court date. Wat 'bout you?" he asked, inquiring about DeJuan's legal situation.

"I gotta do 'bout six months here, then three years on paper," he told Lucci before asking about Shanell. "Have you talked to yo sista lately?" He started thinking about the last time he had seen her.

"Yeah, I talked to her 'bout a week ago. She been keepin some money on tha phone for me. But I jus hit her up when it's necessary, or to check on her to make sure she good. I'm thinkin 'bout crashin wit her when these doors open for me. She don't know yet but I'ma need somewhere to stay til I jump back. You know how these hoes act when a nigga on his dick. It ain't gon take me long to get my bankroll back up though. I just ain't trying to go through that with no bitch when I touch down. I ain't tryna go through that," Lucci explained briefly, looking for a way to ask DeJuan to put him on. It had been all through the jail, even before DeJuan got there, that he was "HIM" in the city.

"I feel ya and I might even be able to help you out when you touch down. I'll rap witcha 'bout it before time comes for you to leave. But look, you got Shanell address? I'ma put her something in the air in tha morning."

"Yeah, no problem. Put it on paper tonight, and I'll have it ready for you when we come out for breakfast," Lucci said. They dapped each other up and went in separate ways to get ready for lockdown.

DeJuan sent the letter out the next morning, and for the next couple of weeks, DeJuan and Shanell shot letters to one another like the phone had yet to be invented, and pen and paper were their only means of communication. He still hadn't been able to get in touch with TyChelle, but with each day passing, and each letter he received from Shanell, he began to think of her less and less. He didn't take her for the type to cut and run. He figured she was strong enough to hold it down, but he also knew that everyone wasn't built for certain things that life threw at them. If he had to cut his losses, then at least he had someone to help him get over the hump of hurt, confusion, and frustration that had been steadily building every time he dialed TyChelle's number.

Somewhere down the line, he convinced Shanell to agree to come see him. Within that time, he had also gotten real cool with Tiger, and even MainSwang to a certain degree, and became part of their little clique.

DeJuan talked about putting them on once they got out, even though he still didn't fully trust MainSwang, and for good reason. He could never overlook a situation, and definitely not theirs, once it reached the point it had with the two of them. He would always keep an eye on him, literally and figuratively.

The three of them had already put together a plan to get on their feet once they got out. Now with DeJuan coming into the fold, they scrapped their former plan and

Qew

was now counting more on DeJuan standing on his word,
to get them up and running straight out the gate.

Chapter 20
Money To Blow

For DeJuan, talking to Shanell face-to-face had been like a breath of fresh air after being underwater, drowning. When she asked if she could come back the following week, there was no way he was going to deny her. He didn't think he had it in him to turn her down, even if he wanted to, which he didn't.

She always seemed to pop up just when he needed someone to talk to, someone who would actually listen instead of let him talk only to respond in the way that they thought he wanted. Regardless of their past ups and downs, DeJuan knew Shanell would never play him like that.

Shanell had never known how to be any other way but genuine.

The entire week leading up to the visitation, DeJuan's mind was filled with thoughts of her. What did she look like now, and more importantly, how much could he confide in her? What would she think if he told her he was at the point of giving up on everything that he had ever known? DeJuan felt like he had really grown in the short time he had been locked up and realized that the stress brought on by the street life was no longer worth the risks he had been taking to provide for his family.

He could now clearly see that those same risks had put his family in danger time and time again. He now saw that there was no winning for anyone playing the game that, for so long, he viewed himself as an all-star at. He was beginning to think that he could really tell Shanell his true feelings. The only question he had was, would she believe him, or figure that it was just a lot of "jail-talk."

At exactly 8:45 am, the C.O. called out, "Williams, visit."

DeJuan had been waiting to hear his name called for about twenty minutes. He couldn't wait to get to the visitation room. The smile on Shanell's face when she first saw him, followed by the embrace she gave him, set the tone for the visit. It turned out to be all that he had hoped for and more. In this case, more didn't necessarily mean anything good. The "more" consisted of him being able to get some things out and off his chest.

He told Shanell that he hadn't talked to TyChelle in more than a week. She told him what she had heard from Crissy… that somebody had shot TyChelle during a robbery and she was in a coma.

As soon as those words left her mouth, DeJuan's mind went into overdrive. There were too many unanswered questions. *Who did it? Where was Lil D? Is he okay? What did they get?*

Before the visit ended, DeJuan gave Shanell J-Smooth's number and asked her to get a message to him to put money on his phone and come see him.

She took a mental note of the number and the message, then assured DeJuan she would handle it. She told him to call her if he needed anything, letting him know that she was willing to step up and do anything she needed to help him.

Heading back to his cell, DeJuan didn't know how to feel, or even what to think. He thought that once he talked to J-Smooth, a lot of the questions would be cleared up. Being honest with himself, DeJuan had to admit the guilt he felt as he lay on his bunk that night, thinking about Shanell.

The following days felt like a roller coaster ride. Through it all, DeJuan kept in touch with Shanell, and by doing so, it kept him in a semi-positive mood, making him feel better. It was as if a doctor had written him a prescription to talk to Shanell once a day, or as needed, because she put a smile on his face every time he did so. He still didn't know the details of what went down at his house, or had heard anything more as to how TyChelle and

Lil D were doing. Every time he thought about the situation, he felt miserable.

He was finally able to talk to Kandace, and aside from letting him know that Lil D was still with her, she couldn't give him any more information about what happened to TyChelle other than what Shanell had already given.

"I talked to Chelle dat morning. She told me she was on her way to get Lil D… I ended up callin her back a few hours later when she hadn't shown up or called. Dat ain't like her, and when she didn't answer, I knew something was wrong," Kandace said.

DeJuan just listened, taking everything in while trying to piece together the little details he had to work with. "Fuck! So don't nobody know nothing?" he said, shaking his head, frustrated. "Have you seen J-Smooth?"

"Yeah, I rode by yo spot that next morning to check on Chelle. Him and Tara was out front arguing 'bout sumn. I asked them what had happened. They said they didn't know and hadn't heard anything," she said.

A couple of days later, Shanell finally got in-touch with J-Smooth.

It was a late Saturday evening. J-Smooth was chilling at Tara's house, high, nodding in front of a sixty-inch plasma TV that was hanging on the wall, when his phone started to vibrate and move across the coffee table. Tara came through the front door just in time to catch it before it hit the floor. She pushed it into J-Smooth's chest, spooking him out of his half-conscious state. She was jealous, she wasn't feeling the way she knew he was.

Grabbing the phone, he looked up at Tara and could tell she was irritated. "Yeah," J-Smooth said. He reached under the couch, pulled out a saucer with about a gram of heroin on it, and placed it on the table for her. He knew exactly why she had an attitude.

"J-Smooth, this is Shanell. I been callin you since yesterday. I went to see DeJuan, and he asked me to call you."

"For real? Wat my nigga up to?" he said, in a slurred tone like everything was peaches and cream on his end, when really it was the exact opposite.

"I think he wants to tell you himself. He just told me to tell you to put some money on your phone and for you to come see him." Shanell said.

"Dat's wat's up. I'ma do tha phone thang now," he said. But his mind was elsewhere. He wondered how DeJuan would react to the fact that he had blown through the stash he had put away. He tried to think of a way to replace what he had jacked off, but since he couldn't come up with a solution, he did what he thought was the next best option and called his heroin dealer.

He didn't want to think about the money he had squandered away any longer and figured he'd escape mentally by self-medicating. He knew DeJuan still had time to kill in the county jail, and he still had enough money to get high with. That was his only logical plan in that moment, and everything else would have to take care of itself when the time came.

Four months had passed since DeJuan left the streets, leaving J-Smooth in control of the operation that once had them both living the life of luxury. During that time, J-Smooth had gotten closer to Tara while he was checking on TyChelle every day, until the day of the robbery. Even after that, he stayed close by to help Tara keep an eye on the house, and help Kandace with Lil D. But there were other reasons he couldn't and didn't want to stray too far away from Tara; their extracurricular activities.

Tara was now hooked on heroin. She did what a lot of women in her position did when they couldn't afford their drug of choice, but wasn't trying to give it up. She found someone that could afford it and introduced it to them; J-Smooth. And once he got a taste, he began to love it more than she did, and that's exactly what she'd hoped would be the outcome.

Once J-Smooth got a taste of the brown monster, Tara no longer had to wonder where her next high would come from. Together, their habit was costing J-Smooth $400-$500 a day. Some days, it was closer to $1,000.

After a couple of months of nodding with Tara, J-Smooth had rifled through $50,000. That's when he turned to trading the coke DeJuan left in the storage, that only he knew about and had access to, for the brown dust he had come to love, even more than the money that, at one point, he cherished more than anything.

Chapter 21
Fresh Out –
The Beginning of the End

DeJuan hadn't talked to TyChelle since the first week or so of being locked up. So when the day came for him to be released, he called Kandace to pick him up.

Kandace and Lil D were waiting outside on 2nd Avenue when DeJuan was released. He had a few pieces of mail in his hand that he dropped when Lil D ran and jumped into his arms.

"Daddy! How come you come outta dere? Auntie said you was outta town," Lil D said as he looked from DeJuan to Kandace and back again.

DeJuan looked at Kandace and shook his head. He didn't agree with her lying to Lil D about his whereabouts. He also knew she didn't agree with how honest DeJuan was with him either. She felt like there were some things Lil D was too young to know.

"Let's jus call it magic, lil dude," DeJuan said, cutting his eye at Kandace.

Kandace took DeJuan and Lil D home so they could spend some time together. She knew they both wanted and needed it.

That evening, they played Spider-Man on the XBOX and watched *Ride Along 2* on DVD. By the end of the movie, Lil D was knocked out, leaving DeJuan alone with his thoughts. That night was the first restless night DeJuan had since Lil D was an infant, even after spending 6 months in jail.

There were rumors about TyChelle's situation, some saying she was in a coma, others saying she was dead. All he knew for sure was that the woman he had planned to marry was nowhere to be found. His safe was empty. His storage unit was cleared out. And J-Smooth was M.I.A.

DeJuan hadn't talked to him at all during the last month of his bid. He kept telling himself there had to be a good reason for the lack of communication, and once they were face-to-face and able to speak freely, J-Smooth would explain.

The situation proved to be more complicated than he had imagined. After being out for nearly two weeks, DeJuan still hadn't seen or heard from J-Smooth. Who he *had* heard from was Lucci. He had been calling nonstop about DeJuan putting him and his crew on. That didn't make anything any better.

DeJuan told Lucci that when he got out, he would set them straight so they wouldn't have to go back to robbing, something they had set their minds to before he had even entered the picture. But that was before DeJuan had come home to see how his six months off the streets had caused the small empire that he had built to crumble to nothing.

On a couple of occasions, while Lil D was at school, DeJuan swung by Talley's to holler at him and Lil Mike, hoping they had heard from, or seen J-Smooth. At the same time, he was trying to decide if jumping back into the streets was what he wanted or needed to do.

When DeJuan left the streets, he made sure that all of his business with Bruce was intact. Even though he knew everything he might need was no more than a phone call away, he was hesitant to make that call and get back to supplying the streets. Thinking about all that he had accomplished and built from the time he devoted to the streets, he felt that he was now back at square one.

When he thought about it, the material things he still had, he knew he could've easily gotten them by working a regular nine-to-five and saving his money. All he really had to show for the long hours he'd given to the streets was a couple of nice cars and the $75,000 that was set aside for Lil D that couldn't be touched for more than a decade.

Looking at the way things were, he knew that he could've gotten all of that without having to spend a day in jail, putting his family at risk, or having TyChelle taken from him. The guilt of having her taken from him because he failed to protect her ate away at him every minute of every day. It sometimes even crept up on him as he slept.

Talley and Lil Mike gave him the same report that everyone else did, that he'd taken the time to listen to. They hadn't heard anything from, or about, J-Smooth other than he had started doing heroin. Like everyone else, they told DeJuan that he'd be the first person they would call if they heard anything. He chilled with them for a few more minutes, finishing the blunt they were smoking before he left to pick up Lil D.

On the way to the school, sitting in his Cadillac, DeJuan pretty much made up his mind to leave the streets alone. He had given too much of himself and hadn't benefited a fraction of what he thought he deserved for his time and dedication. Just as the thought resonated within him, DeJuan pulled up at Lil D's school. He now had a clear mind and plan as to how he was going to live the rest of his life.

He was sitting in the line of cars talking to Shanell on the phone about his revelation when he noticed that more and more cars were leaving, and Lil D still hadn't come out. Cutting the call short, he went inside the school to see why Lil D hadn't been dismissed yet. He let the principal's secretary know that he had been waiting for twenty minutes to pick him up.

What he heard next was disturbing beyond words. She told him that Lil D's *uncle* had picked him up right before lunch.

"Wat tha fuck… sorry, sorry but what do you mean? He doesn't have an uncle," DeJuan said right as his phone vibrated in his pocket.

He ignored his phone focusing on the secretary. "Well, his mother, TyChelle Woods, called earlier and said that her brother would be picking DeJuan up early because of some sort of family emergency."

Overwhelmed by the mention of TyChelle's name and not knowing what was going on, or where Lil D was, DeJuan stormed out of the office. He didn't notice until he was gripping the steering wheel, lost, not knowing what to do or where to go, that his phone was still vibrating. He pulled it from his pocket and answered, full of attitude. "What?"

What he heard in response to his one-word question was enough to send him through the roof of the CTS.

"Three hundred thousand, if you wanna see your son alive again… that's what," The voice on the other end of the phone said.

Chapter 22
"I'm Gon' Kill You!"

It took a few seconds for what was happening to register in DeJuan's head, but once it did, he snapped. "I don't know what you think this is, but I'm gon' kill you if I find out you even thinkin 'bout doin something to my son!"

"Three hunid bands… get it together and wait on my call," is all the caller said before ending the call.

DeJuan pulled away from the school in a blind fury, weighing his options with one thing on his mind: Lil D and getting him home safely. He wished, more than anything at that point, that he had someone to talk to. But not one person came to mind that he could call on to help him fix everything that was either going wrong or had gone wrong in his life.

As he drove, he thought there was no way he could come up with three hundred thousand dollars before whoever had his son called back. He was trying to think of someone whom he might be able to borrow some cash from. The thought of going to the house to get his gun and just showing up with that, once the mystery man called back with the time and place, crossed his mind. Even calling the police entered DeJuan's head. He didn't know how much danger Lil D was actually in and didn't want anything to happen to him. Neither idea lingered in his head once he thought about the man he knew he could turn to in this time of need.

Without giving it a second thought, DeJuan grabbed his phone and searched his contacts for the number to call. As it rang, he began praying desperately that he could get a hold of him. He knew that the man was always busy. He knew how hard it was to get in contact with him and that it was probably only a fifty-fifty chance he was even in town.

When DeJuan heard the raspy tone of the man's voice come through the phone, he felt a wave of relief rush over him so big that had it been in the ocean, it would've caused a tsunami.

"Long time, no hear. How you been, son?" Mr. Johnson asked.

DeJuan and Mr. Johnson had formed a father-son relationship that started the day DeJuan made his first number run for him. Since then, it has grown stronger over the years. Seeing that he had never known who his real father was, he sort of liked having a man to go to about certain things whom he looked up to.

"Shit's fucked up, pops, but I think I can fix it if I can get some of that monopoly money from you." DeJuan said, referring to the counterfeit money that he remembered seeing Mr. Johnson with over the years.

"Yeah… you know I can get that if that's what you need but what's going on?" he asked, curious about how serious DeJuan's situation was.

"I can't rap 'bout it on tha phone, pops. Where can I meet you?"

"I'm at the store right now. How long you talking?"

"ASAP… I'm on tha way." DeJuan hung up and made a U-turn, heading towards 15th Avenue North, where Mr. Johnson owned a small store.

Mr. Johnson had done well for himself in the underworld, running numbers and distributing heroin that he got from Detroit throughout the South. Over the years, he had started turning some of the dirty money into legit businesses. One of the first was the store he bought five years ago.

It was a miracle DeJuan made it to the store in one piece, and without getting a ticket, the way he was driving. He jumped out of the Cadillac and headed towards the store.

When he walked inside, Dolla Bill, an older man who worked for Mr. Johnson for years, looked up and said, "Wat up D-Money… I heard you was out. What's good?"

"Not a whole lot," DeJuan said, looking towards Mr. Johnson.

Mr. Johnson got up from behind the counter and headed for the door DeJuan had just walked through. He told Dolla Bill to keep an eye on things while he stepped out.

Once they were outside, Mr. Johnson turned to DeJuan. "What's up, son?" he said.

DeJuan leaned against an Escalade he was parked behind as if he had the keys to it, opposed to the CTS that he had stepped out of, and fired up a Newport. He went into details about the kidnapping and ransom as he knew them.

Mr. Johnson listened intently, smoking a Kool 100, trying to keep his composure. He stayed quiet the whole time to allow DeJuan to make the decision on how he wanted to handle the situation.

When it was all said and done, the decision was simple. DeJuan was going to pack some clothes, pass off the counterfeit to whoever had Lil D, then hit the highway with his son, leaving everything else behind.

DeJuan had family in Indianapolis that he and Lil D could stay with until he got them into a place of their own. That was his plan, but Mr. Johnson had other plans in mind, but still obliged DeJuan's wishes. He gave DeJuan $300,000 in counterfeit, and another $20,000 that was real, and told him to call him once he got Lil D, so he knew they were good before they left town.

Once everything was agreed upon, they went back into the store for a few more words and to get the small duffel bag containing the fake money and two envelopes, which held ten thousand each. DeJuan put the duffel bag in the trunk and the envelopes of real money in the glove compartment before pulling off.

As he pulled up to the house, he got the call he was waiting for. He was still in disbelief about the situation altogether. The kidnappers agreed to meet an hour later to make the exchange. They told DeJuan to be at Centennial Park and drop the money off by the flyer jet. Once the drop was made and the money was accounted for, he would get another call telling him where to pick up Lil D. His only request to them was that he got to hear his son's voice.

Lil D was put on the phone, and not only did he say he hadn't been hurt, but he went on to say that the men he was with were nice. DeJuan figured his son didn't know the circumstances of why he had been picked up from school by the stranger that was being nice to him, and if he had things his way, he would never need to know or have to worry about them.

After talking to his son briefly, DeJuan did everything he was told to do and was rewarded with a call telling him to go to the playground, where Lil D would be at the swing set. He felt like he was in a dream. Pulling up to the playground, Lil D jumped out of the swing and was running towards him before he was even out of the car.

"Daddy, me and uncle T was talking 'bout you. He said you was finna come get me," Lil D said, looking back to where he was just swinging. "He was just ova dere," he added, pointing to the picnic table a few feet away from the swings.

"Don't worry 'bout him, lil dude. You wit me now, and we finna take a trip," DeJuan said as he hurried Lil D into the car. He felt a hundred times better with his son safely buckled in beside him, but his plans hadn't changed. He was still set on getting away from Nashville.

DeJuan pulled out of the park into the evening traffic that was always a mess at that time on West End Avenue. He turned left and headed for I-65, making only one stop, to fill up the tank and grab some snacks for the road before getting to the interstate. They drove long enough for Lil D to doze off until DeJuan put in a T.I. CD and turned it up, jarring Lil D out of his sleep.

As the bass came through the speakers, the vibration that went through the car caused the rearview mirror to fall off. DeJuan reached for it, trying to put it back but decided not. He took it as a clear sign that he was doing the right thing by leaving, and he had no reason to look back.